The HEART of a SOLDIER

The HEART *of a* SOLDIER

Intimate
Wartime Letters from
General GEORGE E. PICKETT *C.S.A.*
to His Wife

Stan Clark Military Books
Gettysburg, Pennsylvania

Reprinted in 1995 by:

STAN CLARK MILITARY BOOKS
915 Fairview Avenue
Gettysburg, Pennsylvania 17325
(717) 337-1728

ISBN: 1-879664-24-0

Printed and bound in the United States of America

FOREWORD

FOR half a century these letters have lain locked away from the world, the lines fading upon the yellowed pages, their every word enshrined in the heart of the noble woman to whom they were written. To her they came filled with the thunder of guns, the lightning of unsheathed swords, the tumultuous rage in the heart of the storm; but through them all the radiance of a pure devotion outshone the battle flash and the lyric of a great love rose above the cannon's roar. To their possessor, naturally, these letters are sacred and they are given to the world with great reluctance. It is only the thought of the inspiration that they can bring to lives less glorious than that of him who penned them, of the courage they can instill into hearts less brave, that has led their owner to share them with the world.

Through the medium of this volume, which is hereby dedicated to the Great Soldier and True Man who supplied its contents, these letters are given, out of the hands of one who has cherished them tenderly for many years, into the keeping of all those who honor courage, loyalty and the love of man for woman.

C O N T E N T S

PART ONE

PART TWO

C O N T E N T S

Continued

C O N T E N T S

Continued

C O N T E N T S

Continued

For the Introduction to this book, credit is due to McClure's Magazine, in which the article first appeared.

I L L U S T R A T I O N S

By FRANKLIN BOOTH

Do you remember, my Sally, how many times we said Good-bye that evening?

"The enemy is there, General, and I am going to strike him," said Marse Robert in his firm, quiet voice.

Two lines of their infantry were driven back; two lines of guns were taken — and no support came.

You must have been up all night, my prettice, to have made up and sent out such a basket of goodies. My, I tell you, it all tasted good.

*Do you remember, my Sally,
how many times we said good-
bye that evening?—Page 80.*

The HEART *of a* SOLDIER

An Introductory Chapter
from the One to Whom these Letters
were Written

EARLY in life's morning I knew and loved him, and from my first meeting with him to the end, I always called him "Soldier"—"My Soldier." I was a wee bit of a girl at that first meeting. I had been visiting my grandmother, when whooping-cough broke out in the neighborhood, and she took me off to Old Point Comfort to visit her friend, Mrs. Boykin, the sister of John Y. Mason. I could dance and sing and play games and was made much of by the other children and their parents there, till I suddenly developed the cough, then I was shunned and isolated.

I could not understand the change. I would press my face against the ball-room window-panes and watch the merry-making inside and my little heart would almost break. One morning, while playing alone on the beach, I saw an officer lying on the sand reading, under the shelter of an umbrella. I had noticed him several times, always apart from the others, and very sad. I could imagine but one reason for his desolation and in pity for him, I crept under his umbrella to ask him if he, too, had the whooping-cough. He smiled and answered no; but as I still persisted he drew me to him, telling me that he had lost someone who was dear to him and he was very lonely.

And straightway, without so much as a by-your-leave, I promised to take the place of his dear one and to comfort him in his loss. Child as I was, I believe I lost my heart to him on the spot. At all events, I crept from under the umbrella pledged to Lieutenant George E. Pickett, U. S. A., for life and death, and I still hold most sacred a little ring and locket that he gave me on that day.

It is small wonder that this first picture of

him is among the most vivid still; the memory
of him as he lay stretched in the shade of
the umbrella, not tall, and rather slender, but
very graceful, and perfect in manly beauty.
With childish appreciation, I particularly noticed his very small hands and feet. He had
beautiful gray eyes that looked at me through
sunny lights—eyes that smiled with his lips.
His mustache was gallantly curled. His hair
was exactly the color of mine, dark brown,
and long and wavy, in the fashion of the time.
The neatness of his dress attracted even a
child's admiration. His shirt-front of the
finest white linen, was in soft puffs and ruffles, and the sleeves were edged with hem-
stitched thread cambric ruffles. He would
never, to the end of his life, wear the stiff linen
collars and cuffs and stocks which came into
fashion among men. While he was at West
Point he paid heavily in demerits for ob-
stinacy in refusing to wear the regulation
stock. Only when the demerits reached the
danger-point would he temporarily give up
his soft necktie.

It was under that umbrella, in the days that
followed, that I learned, while he guided my

3

hand, to make my first letters and spell my first words. They were "Sally" and "Soldier." I remember, too, the songs he used to sing me in the clear, rich voice of which his soldiers were so fond, frequently accompanying himself on the guitar. He kept a diary of those days and after the war it was returned to him from San Juan by the British officer who occupied the island conjointly with him before the opening of the war. I have it now in my possession.

Three years after our first meeting I saw my Soldier again. He had just received his commission as captain, and was recruiting his company at Fortress Monroe, before sailing for San Juan. The first real sorrow of my life was when I watched the *St. Louis* go out to sea with my Soldier on board, bound around the Horn to Puget Sound, where he was stationed at Fort Bellingham, which I thought must be farther than the end of the world. Forty thousand Indians had risen against the settlers. For two years he was in the thick of it, and greatly distinguished himself, but he did even better after the Indians were suppressed, for he made them his friends,

4

learned their languages, built school-houses for them and taught them, and they called him *Nesika Tyee*—Our Chief. One old Indian chief insisted upon making him a present of one of his children. He translated the Lord's Prayer and some of our hymns and patriotic songs into their jargon and taught the Indians to sing them. He taught me some of them afterward. Years later, one night after the Civil War, while we were exiles in Montreal, General Pickett and I were singing a hymn in Chinook to put our baby to sleep, when a voice in the next room joined us. At the close of the hymn a stranger came and spoke to my Soldier in Chinook. When he left, he invited us to the theater where he was playing. He was William Florence, and he gave me my first taste of the pleasures of the drama.

Following the Indian war, the quarrel with the British over the ownership of San Juan Island reached a white heat, and on the night of July 26, 1859, my Soldier, with sixty-eight men, was sent from the mainland to take possession. They were none too soon, for when morning dawned there were five British war-ships off the coast, with nineteen hundred and forty men ready to land. They proposed joint occupation, but Captain Pickett replied:

"I cannot allow joint occupation until so ordered by my commanding general."

The English captain said: "I have a thousand men ready to land to-night."

Captain Pickett replied: "Captain, if you undertake it, I will fight you as long as I have a man."

"I shall land at once," said the British offi-cer.

"If you will give me forty-eight hours, till I hear from my commanding officer, my or-ders may be countermanded. If you don't you must be responsible for the bloodshed that will follow."

"Not one minute," was the English cap-tain's reply.

My Soldier gave orders for the drawing up of his men in lines on the hill facing the beach where the English must land.

"We will make a Bunker Hill of it, and don't be afraid of their big guns," he said.

In his official report General Harney said: "So satisfied were the British officers that Captain Pickett would carry out this course, that they hesitated."

The United States retained the Island and my Soldier remained in command until the outbreak of the Civil War. But when Virginia passed the Ordinance of Secession he resigned his commission and recognizing the claims of his native state, joined his fortunes with those of the Southland, although, like many others who fought as bravely against the national government as in happier times they had fought for it, he loved the Union and every star in that flag which he had so often borne to victory.

My Soldier reached Richmond September 13, 1861, and at once enlisted as a private. The next day he was given a commission as captain, a short time later promoted to a colonelcy, and early in 1862 received his commission as brigadier-general. In June, while leading his brigade in a charge at Gaines's Mill, he was severely wounded in the shoulder, but refused to leave the field, ordering Dr. Chancellor to extract the bullet on the field. The surgeon remonstrated, but he said:

"My men need me here, Doctor. Fix me now."

He was finally carried off, but was back with his brigade two months before he was able to draw a sleeve over the wounded arm.

Time has not lessened the fame of Pickett's Charge at Gettysburg, and it never will; for the changes that have taken place in the science of war leave no possibility that future history will produce its counterpart. Truly, "the first day of the terrible three at Gettysburg was an accident, the second a blunder" and the third the greatest tragedy that has ever been played upon the stage of war. With its imperishable glory—overshadowing all other events in martial history, notwithstanding its appalling disaster—is linked forever the name of my Soldier.

Down the slope into the smoke-filled valley
the devoted men followed him as he rode in
advance upon his black war-horse. Their
ranks were thinned and torn and shattered by
the tempest of lead which from every side
was turned on them. Smoke and flame sur-
rounded them. But from the rear the men
sprang to fill the gaps in front as they pressed
after their leader through the tempest of iron.
Five thousand Virginians followed him at
the start; but when the Southern flag floated
on the ridge, in less than half an hour, not two
thousand were left to rally beneath it, and
those for only one glorious, victory-intoxi-
cated moment. They were not strong enough
to hold the position they had so dearly won;
and, broken-hearted, even at the very moment
of his immortal triumph, my Soldier led his
remaining men down the slope again. He
dismounted and walked beside the stretcher
upon which General Kemper, one of his officers, was being carried, fanning him and
speaking cheerfully to comfort him in his suffering. When he reached Seminary Ridge
again and reported to General Lee, his face

9

was wet with tears as he pointed to the crimson valley and said:

"My noble division lies there!"

"General Pickett," said the commander, "you and your men have covered yourselves with glory."

"Not all the glory in the world, General Lee," my Soldier replied, "could atone for the widows and orphans this day has made."

Soon after the great battle my Soldier confided to his corps commander his intention of marrying, and asked for a furlough. General Longstreet replied that they were not granting furloughs then, but added, with the twinkle in his eye which those who knew him so well will remember: "I might detail you for special duty and you could, of course, stop off and get married if you wanted to."

In old St. Paul's Church in Petersburg, September 15, 1863, we were married, while the bells rang out the chimes that still make music from that old belfry and are yet known as "Pickett's Chimes." In the throng which crowded the church and extended to the sidewalk were hundreds whose mourning garb attested to the costly sacrifice which Petersburg had given to the South. Many hands were reached out to greet my Soldier, and from the lips of many a black-robed mother came the words: "My son was with you at Gettysburg —God bless you!" A salute of a hundred guns announced the marriage; cheers followed us, and chimes and bands and bugles played as we left for our wedding reception in Richmond.

The food supply of the South was reduced to narrow limits then. Salt was reclaimed from the earth under smoke-houses. Guests at distinguished functions were regaled with ice-cream made of frozen buttermilk sweetened with sorghum. But friends of the general had almost worked miracles to prepare a wedding supper. It was sora season, and those little birds had been killed at night with paddles—the South being not much richer in ammunition than in edibles—and contributed so lavishly to our banquet that it was always afterward known as "the wedding sora supper." Our wedding present from Mrs. Lee was a fruit-cake, and Bishop Dudley's mother sent a black cake she had been saving for her golden wedding. Little bags of salt and sugar were sent as presents. The army was in camp near by, and all the men at the reception, except President Davis, his cabinet, and a few clergymen, came in full uniform, officers and privates as well. We returned without delay to Petersburg, that being my Soldier's headquarters.

In early May, General Butler, with thirty thousand men, came down upon Petersburg, defended by only six hundred. They held the place till half-starved and ragged reinforcements were hurried in from every direction. We women carried the despatches, and cooked the food and took it to the men at the guns. The roar of the cannon and the shriek of shot and shell filled our ears day and night. At train-time we would go to the station and send up cheer after cheer to welcome the train from its short trip out into the country, hoping to blind the Yankees to the fact that it brought in only the half-starved railroad men. During the entire week, until he had Butler safely "bottled up at Petersburg," my Soldier did not sleep, and the only times I saw him were when I carried his bread and soup and coffee out to him. It was just as it had been when he started for Cemetery Hill at Gettysburg. He would never stop till he had accomplished his work. After Pickett's Division had retaken Bermuda Hundred the following summer, General Anderson, commanding Longstreet's Corps, wrote to General Lee: "We tried very hard to stop Pickett and his men from capturing the breastworks of the enemy, but we could not do it."

The devotion of General Pickett's men to him has often been recounted as something phenomenal. It was equaled only by his devotion to them. Very near the end of the war, when the army had subsisted on nothing but corn for many days, as my Soldier was riding toward Sailor's Creek, a woman ran out of a house and handed him something to eat. He carried it in his hand as he rode on. Presently he came upon a soldier lying behind a log, and spoke to him. The man looked up, revealing a boyish face, scarcely more than a child's—thin and pale.

"What's the matter?" asked my Soldier.

"I'm starving, General," the boy replied. "I couldn't help it. I couldn't keep up, so I just lay down here to die."

"Take this," handing the boy his luncheon; "and when you have eaten and rested, go on back home. It would only waste another life for you to go on."

The boy took the food eagerly, but replied: "No, Marse George. If I get strength enough to go at all, I'll follow you to the last." He did, for he was killed a few days later at Sailor's Creek.

I was in Richmond when my Soldier fought the awful battle of Five Forks, Richmond surrendered, and the surging sea of fire swept the city. News of the fate of Five Forks had reached us, and the city was full of rumors that General Pickett was killed. I did not believe them. I knew he would come back, he had told me so. But they were very anxious hours. The day after the fire, there was a sharp rap at the door. The servants had all run away. The city was full of northern troops, and my environment had not taught me to love them. The fate of other cities had awakened my fears for Richmond. With my baby on my arm, I answered the knock, opened the door and looked up at a tall, gaunt, sad-faced man in ill-fitting clothes. who, with the accent of the North, asked:

"Is this George Pickett's place?"

"Yes, sir," I answered, "but he is not here."

"I know that, ma'am," he replied, "but I just wanted to see the place. I am Abraham Lincoln."

"The President!" I gasped.

The stranger shook his head and said:

"No, ma'am; no, ma'am; just Abraham Lincoln; George's old friend."

"I am George Pickett's wife and this is his baby," was all I could say. I had never seen Mr. Lincoln but remembered the intense love and reverence with which my Soldier always spoke of him.

My baby pushed away from me and reached out his hands to Mr. Lincoln, who took him in his arms. As he did so an expression of rapt, almost divine, tenderness and love lighted up the sad face. It was a look that I have never seen on any other face. My baby opened his mouth wide and insisted upon giving his father's friend a dewy infantile kiss. As Mr. Lincoln gave the little one back to me, shaking his finger at him playfully, he said:

"Tell your father, the rascal, that I forgive him for the sake of that kiss and those bright eyes."

He turned and went down the steps, talking to himself, and passed out of my sight forever, but in my memory those intensely human eyes, that strong, sad face, have a perpetual abiding place—that face which puzzled all artists but revealed itself to the intuitions of a little child, causing it to hold out its hands to be taken and its lips to be kissed.

It was through Mr. Lincoln that my Soldier, as a lad of seventeen, received his appointment to West Point. Mr. Lincoln was at that time associated in law practice with George Pickett's uncle, Mr. Andrew Johnston, a distinguished lawyer and scholar, who was very anxious that his nephew should follow in his footsteps and study for the law—an ambition which, it is needless to say, my Soldier did not share. He confided his perplexities to Mr. Lincoln, who was very fond of the boy; and the great statesman went at once to work to secure his appointment.

After Richmond's fall I anxiously awaited my Soldier's return, and at last one morning I caught the familiar clatter of the hoofs of his little thoroughbred chestnut which he always rode when he came home, and the sound of his voice saying: "Whoa, Lucy, whoa, little girl."

He gave his staff a farewell breakfast at our home. They did not once refer to the past, but each wore a blue strip tied like a sash around his waist. It was the old headquarter's flag, which they had saved from the surrender and torn into strips, that each might keep one in sad memory. After breakfast he went to the door, and from a white rose-bush which his mother had planted cut a bud for each. He put one in my hair and pinned one to the coat of each of his officers. Then for the first time the tears came, and the men who had been closer than brothers for four fearful years, clasped hands in silence and parted.

Ever since the Mexican War General Grant had been a dear friend of my Soldier. At the time our first baby was born the two armies were encamped facing each other and they often swapped coffee and tobacco under flags of truce. On the occasion of my son's birth bonfires were lighted in celebration all along Pickett's line. Grant saw them and sent scouts to learn the cause. When they reported, he said to General Ingalls:

"Haven't we some kindling on this side of the line? Why don't we strike a light for the young Pickett?"

In a little while bonfires were flaming from the Federal line. A few days later there was taken through the lines a baby's silver service, engraved: "To George E. Pickett, Jr., from his father's friends, U. S. Grant, Rufus Ingalls, George Suckley."

It was through their courtesy, at the close of the war, that we were taken from Richmond down the James to my father's old home at Chuckatuck. But we were not allowed to remain long at peace. General Ingalls warned my Soldier that General Butler was making speeches against him in Congress, and urged that he would be safer on foreign ground. Though he did not believe it, he reluctantly consented to go. He mounted Lucy and rode to the station. It was a pathetic incident that, just as the train moved out, the chestnut thoroughbred lay down and died.

We had been in Canada almost a year when General Grant, learning of our exile, wrote to us to return, saying that his cartel with General Lee should be kept, if it required another war to make it good. We went back to our dear old place, Turkey Island, on the James River, and built a little cottage in the place of the magnificent mansion which had been sacked and burned by order of General Butler. I once asked my Soldier why it was called Turkey Island. He replied that there were two good reasons; one was that it was not an island, the other that there were never any turkeys there. Everything, even the monument in the family cemetery, had been destroyed, but it was home. We loved it. My Soldier was always passionately fond of flowers, and our garden was an unfailing delight to us both.

He tried to turn his sword into a plowshare, but he was not expert with plowshares; and, worse, he constantly received applications for employment from old comrades no more skilled than he. All were made welcome, though they might not be able to distinguish a rake from a rail fence or tell whether potatoes grew on trees or on trellised vines. They would rise at any hour that pleased them, linger over breakfast, and then go out to the fields. If the sun were too hot or the wind too cold, they would come back, to sit on the veranda or around the fire till dinner was ready. There were generals, colonels, majors, captains, lieutenants, privates— all of one rank now; and he who desired a graphic history of the four years' war needed only to listen to the conversation of the agricultural army at Turkey Island. But the inevitable came; resources were in time exhausted, and proprietor and assistants were forced to seek other fields.

The Khedive of Egypt offered my Soldier the position of general in his army, but he declined. When General Grant became President, he entertained us as his guests at the White House, and one of my keenest memories is of President Grant and my Soldier as they stood facing each other in the White House office the last day of our visit. Grant's hand was on the shoulder of my Soldier, and they were looking earnestly into each other's eyes. Grant, ever faithful to his friends, had been urging my Soldier to accept the marshalship of the State of Virginia. Pickett, sorely as he needed the appointment, knew the demands upon Grant, and that his acceptance would create criticism and enemies for the President. He shook his head, saying:

"You can't afford to do this for me, Sam, and I can't afford to take it."

"I can afford to do anything I please," said Grant. My Soldier still shook his head, but the deep emotion of his heart shone in his tear-dimmed eyes, and in Grant's, as they silently grasped each other's hands and then walked away in opposite directions and looked out of separate windows, while I stole away.

My Soldier was urged to accept the position with Generals Beauregard and Early in connection with the Louisiana Lottery. There was a large salary attached to it, but he said there was not money enough in the world to induce him to lend his name to it.

When he was offered the governorship of Virginia, he said that he never again wanted to hold any office, and would be glad to see Kemper, his old brigadier, made governor. Kemper was the only one of Pickett's brigadiers who came out of the battle of Gettysburg, and he was wounded and maimed for life. He was elected governor, and as he was a bachelor, my Soldier and I often assisted him at his receptions.

For himself, my Soldier finally accepted the general agency for the South of the Washington Life Insurance Company, and held the office till his death. The headquarters were at Richmond. I always went with him on his trips, and we spent our summers in the Virginia mountains.

External conditions as well as natural instincts made my Soldier's life one of deep and tragic earnestness. He was always grave and dignified, but he was fond of jokes, especially if they were on me. Once, when he was leaving home for an absence of some length, he asked how much money I would need. I made a laborious calculation, and named a sum which he promptly doubled. He had not been gone long when I remembered an obligation, and telegraphed him that I had underestimated the amount. By the next mail came a check carefully made payable to "Mrs. Oliver Twist." I had to indorse it in that way, and he always carried the cheque in his pocket afterward for my benefit. I have it now.

At the wedding breakfast given for General Magruder's niece at the mansion of the governor-general of Canada, the governor asked my Soldier to what he attributed the failure of the Confederates at Gettysburg. With a twinkle in his eyes, he replied, "Well, I think the Yankees had a little something to do with it."

In the summer of 1875, when we were prepared to start for White Sulphur Springs, my Soldier was suddenly called to Norfolk. Very much against his advice, I insisted on accompanying him. It was fortunate, for after two days of anxious work he fell ill, and died there. The evening he was dying, the doctor wanted to give him an anodyne, but he said:

"Doctor, you say that I must die. I want to go in my right mind. I would rather suffer pain and know. Please leave me now. I do not want anybody but my wife."

The longest procession of mourners ever known in Virginia followed him to his grave on Gettysburg Hill, in beautiful Hollywood.

General Longstreet has written of my Soldier:

"I first met him as a cadet at West Point, in the heyday of his bright young manhood, in 1842. Upon graduating, he was assigned to the regiment to which I had been promoted, the Eighth United States Infantry, and Lieutenant Pickett served gallantly with us continuously until, for meritorious service, he was promoted captain in 1856. He served with distinguished valor in all the battles of General Scott in Mexico, including the siege of Vera Cruz, and was always conspicuous for gallantry. He was the first to scale the parapets of Chapultepec on the 13th of September, 1847, and was the brave American who unfurled our flag over the castle as the enemy's troops retreated, firing at the splendid Pickett as he floated our victorious colors.

"In memory I can see him, of medium height, of graceful build, dark, glossy hair, worn almost to his shoulders in curly waves, of wondrous pulchritude and magnetic presence, as he gallantly rode from me on that memorable third day of July, 1863, saying, in obedience to the imperative order to which I could only bow assent, 'I will lead my division forward, General Longstreet.' He was devoted to his martial profession . . .

"His greatest battle was really at Five Forks, April 1, 1865, where his plans and operations were masterful and skillful. If they had been executed as he designed them there might have been no Appomattox, and despite the disparity of overwhelming numbers, a brilliant victory would have been his if reinforcements which he had every reason to expect had opportunely reached him; but they were not ordered in season and did not join the hard-pressed Pickett until night, when his position had long since been attacked by vastly superior numbers with repeating rifles.

"He was of an open, frank, and genial temperament, but he felt very keenly the distressing calamities entailed upon the beloved sunny South by the results of the war; yet, with the characteristic fortitude of a soldier, he bowed with resignation to the inevitable, gracefully accepted the situation, recognized the duty of the unfortunate to accept the

26

results in no querulous spirit, and felt his obligation to share its effects.

"No word of blame, or censure even, of his superior officers ever escaped Pickett's lips, but he nevertheless felt profoundly the sacrifice of his gallant soldiers whom he so loved. At Five Forks he had a desperate but a fighting chance, and if any soldier could have snatched victory from defeat, it was the intrepid Pickett, and it was cruel to leave that brilliant and heroic leader and his Spartan band to the same hard straits they so nobly met at Gettysburg. At Five Forks Pickett lost more men in thirty minutes than we lost, all told, in the recent Spanish-American war from bullets, wounds, sickness, or any other casualty, showing the unsurpassed bravery with which Pickett fought, and the tremendous odds and insuperable disadvantages under and against which this incomparable soldier so bravely contended; but with George E. Pickett, whether fighting under the stars and stripes at Chapultepec, or under the stars and bars at Gettysburg, duty was his polar star, and with him duty was above consequences, and at a crisis, he would throw them overboard."

General McClellan has said:

"Perhaps there is no doubt that he was the best infantry soldier developed on either side during the Civil War. His friends and admirers are by no means confined to the Southern people or soldiers to whom he gave his heart and best affections and of whom he was so noble a type, but throughout the North and on the Pacific coast, where he long served, his friends and lovers are legion.

THE HEART OF A SOLDIER

"He was of the purest type of the perfect soldier, possessing manly beauty in the highest degree; a mind large and capable of taking in the bearings of events under all circumstances; of that firm and dauntless texture of soul that no danger or shock of conflict could appall or confuse; full of that rare magnetism which could infuse itself into masses of men and cause any mass under his control to act as one; his perception clear; his courage of that rare proof which rose to the occasion; his genius for war so marked that his companions all knew that his mind worked clearer under fire and in the 'deadly and imminent breach,' than even at mess-table or in the merry bivouac, where his genial and kindly comradeship and his perfect breeding as a gentleman made him beloved of his friends.

"He will live in history as nearer to Light Horse Harry, of the Revolution, than any other of the many heroes produced by Old Virginia—his whole history, when told, as it will be by some of the survivors of Pickett's men, will reveal a modern type of the Chevalier Bayard, *sans peur et sans reproche.* . . .

"Could he have had his wish, he had died amid the roar of battle. No man of our age has better illustrated the aptitude for war of his class of our country, and with these talents for war was united the truest and sweetest nature. No man of his time was more beloved of women, of men and of soldiers. He was to the latter a rigid disciplinarian and at the same time the soldier's friend. Virginia will rank him in her roll of fame with Lee, with Johnston, with Jackson they love as Stonewall; and mourners for the noble and gallant gentleman, the able and accomplished soldier, are legion."

These were the tributes of friend and enemy—if any man, though he fought him on the field of battle, could be called his enemy. Rivers of blood did not quench the flames of the campfires of Mexico and the West. My Soldier's comrades under the old flag were still his comrades through the crucial test of that most deadly warfare, a conflict between the opposing sections of the same country.

To me the legacy of love that he left in his letters and in the memories of his daily life is greater than any riches earth could give. The nobility of soul with which he met the problems that come to men in the arena of the world is a treasured possession in my heart even greater than his magnificent heroism on the field of battle. The radiance of the stars in the blue sky of peace eclipse the crimson glow of the fiery comet of war. The heart of "My Soldier" is mine to-day as it was

THE HEART OF A SOLDIER

in that long-gone yesterday when I awaited the messages that link the battlefield with to-morrow's Eternal Harmony.

LA SALLE CORBELL PICKETT.

PART ONE

In the early days of the Long Struggle

AT the time when these letters begin, the General (then Captain Pickett, U. S. A.) was stationed at Fort Bellingham in the northwest. Before leaving Virginia, he had become engaged to "Little Miss Sally" Corbell, who during his absence was fitting herself at school to be a soldier's wife. The summons to arms in the cause of the seceding states was late in reaching the Captain at his far-away post, and he, being in the dark as to the course of events, was even more tardy to respond; but when the news came telling of the withdrawal of his native state from the Union he resigned his commission immediately and cast his lot with that of the Confederacy.

The letters in this part give many vivid glimpses of the armies in action, as they do of the lighter side of a soldier's life, during the first year and a half of the War. There are lapses of weeks—even months—between them, due to the fact that some are missing; others, whose pages time has stained, are undecipherable, and in still other instances the fortunes of war kept the General so near his sweetheart that letters were not needed to carry to her the tale of his love.

THE HEART OF A SOLDIER

I

In Which the General Tells Why He Sided With the South

SEVERAL weeks ago I wrote quite a long letter from far-away San Francisco to a very dear little girl, and told her that a certain soldier who wears one of her long, silken ringlets next his heart was homeward bound and that he hoped a line of welcome would meet him on his arrival in his native state. He told her of the difficulties he had experienced in being relieved from his post, of how sorry he was to sheathe the sword which had helped to bring victory to the country for which he had fought, and how sorry he was to say good-by to his little command and to part from his faithful and closest companion, his dog, and his many dear friends; but sorrier still for the existing circumstances which

made this severance necessary. He told her
many things for which, with him, she will be
sorry, and some of which he hopes will make
her glad. He is troubled by finding no answer to this long letter which, having at that
time no notion of the real conditions here, he
is afraid was written too freely by far.

No, my child, I had no conception of the
intensity of feeling, the bitterness and hatred
toward those who were so lately our friends
and are now our enemies. I, of course, have
always strenuously opposed disunion, not as
doubting the right of secession, which was
taught in our text-book at West Point, but as
gravely questioning its expediency. I believed that the revolutionary spirit which in-
fected both North and South was but a passing
phase of fanaticism which would perish under
the rebuke of all good citizens, who would
surely unite in upholding the Constitution;
but when that great assembly, composed of
ministers, lawyers, judges, chancellors, states-
men, mostly white haired men of thought, met
in South Carolina and when their districts
were called crept noiselessly to the table in

the center of the room and affixed their signatures to the parchment on which the ordinance of secession was inscribed, and when in deathly silence, spite of the gathered multitude, General Jamison arose and without preamble read: "The ordinance of secession has been signed and ratified; I proclaim the State of South Carolina an independent sovereignty," and lastly, when my old boyhood's friend called for an invasion, it was evident that both the advocates and opponents of secession had read the portents aright.

You know, my little lady, some of those cross-stitched mottoes on the cardboard samplers which used to hang on my nursery wall, such as, "He who provides not for his own household is worse than an infidel" and "Charity begins at home," made a lasting impression upon me; and while I love my neighbor, i. e., my country, I love my household, i. e., my state, *more,* and I could not be an infidel and lift my sword against my own kith and kin, even though I do believe, my most wise little counselor and confidante, that the measure of American greatness can be achieved only under one flag, and I fear, alas, there can never again reign for either of us the true spirit of national unity, whether divided under two flags or united under one.

We did not tarry even for a day in 'Frisco, but under assumed names my friend, Sam Barron, and I sailed for New York, where we arrived on the very day that Sam's father, Commodore Barron, was brought there a prisoner, which fact was proclaimed aloud by the pilot amid cheers of the passengers and upon our landing heralded by the newsboys with more cheers. Poor Sam had a hard fight to hide his feelings and to avoid arrest. We separated as mere ship acquaintances, and went by different routes to meet again, as arranged, at the house of Doctor Paxton, a Southern sympathizer and our friend.

On the next day we left for Canada by the earliest train. Thence we made our perilous way back south again, barely escaping arrest several times, and finally arrived in dear old Richmond, September 13th, just four days ago. I at once enlisted in the army and the

following day was commissioned Captain.
But so bitter is the feeling here that my being
unavoidably delayed so long in avowing my
allegiance to my state has been most cruelly
and severely criticized by friends—yes, and
even relatives, too.

Now, little one, if you had the very faintest
idea how happy a certain captain in the C. S.
A. (My, but that "C" looks queer!) would be
to look into your beautiful, soul-speaking eyes
and hear your wonderfully musical voice, I
think you would let him know by wire where
he could find you. I shall almost listen for
the electricity which says, "I am at ——.
Come." I know that you will have mercy on
your devoted

SOLDIER.

Richmond, September 17, 1861.

II

Written After a Light Skirmish With the Enemy

YOUR welcome note gladdened my droop-
ing spirits last evening. How can I
thank you for the token?[1] I shall always
cherish it, my darling. I sent a short note to
you via Petersburg to Wakefield. I sincerely
trust you received it, as in it I advised you not
to come down into this part of the country.
The Yankees are burning everything they can
reach, and God only knows what excesses they
may commit on the defenseless, should they
have the power. So much troubled am I
about you, that I send this by a courier of my
own, that he may deliver it to you in person
(how I wish I were the courier). I'm afraid
you will only expose yourself needlessly to

[1] A wreath and stars, which she had embroidered for his
collar.

harm. I don't know when I shall see you, but I should be nearly as far from you as at present. At any rate, I should be worse than miserable did I know you were so near these now apparently infuriated beings.

Alas, my darling, as the Indian says when despondent, "My heart is on the ground." The enemy has been strongly reënforced, and the town is one network of batteries and entrenchments. I have had two little brushes with them, running them into their works both times—the first one yesterday week. I was ordered to make a reconnaissance in force, which was done by a part of Armistead's Brigade, and in so doing we got under a concentrated fire of about sixteen guns and had as jolly a little time of it for about fifteen minutes as I ever saw. Parrot and round shot were about as thick as the ticks are, and their name is legion. However, the object was effected, and we have lost altogether only about seventy-five men from my division.

Haven't you some relatives living this side of the Blackwater—a Captain Phillips of the 3rd? Write me, my dearest. Two long,

THE HEART OF A SOLDIER

weary weeks since I drank comfort from those bright eyes—to me a *year* of anxiety.

Your devoted and miserable

SOLDIER.

New Somerton Road, April 21, 1862.

III

Concerning Legitimate Warfare, Secession and the Mishaps of an Old Major of Artillery

MY heart beat with joy this morning when Captain Peacock returned to camp, bringing me your beautiful letter—beautiful because it was the echo of a pure spirit and a radiant soul. I am humbly grateful, my little girl, for this loyal devotion which you give me—your Soldier. Let us pray to our dear Heavenly Father to spare us to each other and give us strength to bear cheerfully this enforced separation. I know that it cannot be long, and that sooner or later our flag will float over the seas of the world, for our cause is right and just.

Why, my Sally, all that we ask is a separation from people of contending interests, who love us as a nation as little as we love them, the dissolution of a union which has lost its holiness, to be let alone and permitted to sit under our own vine and fig tree and eat our figs peeled and dried or fresh or pickled, just as we choose. The enemy is our enemy because he neither knows nor understands us, and yet will not let us part in peace and be neighbors, but insists on fighting us to make us one with him, forgetting that both slavery and secession were his own institutions. The North is fighting for the Union, and we—for home and fireside. All the men I know and love in the world—comrades and friends, both North and South—are exposed to hardships and dangers, and are fighting on one side or the other, and each for that which he knows to be right.

Speaking of fighting, Captain Peacock this morning brings us the news that the daring, fearless —— has again won—shall I say, a victory? No, not victory. Victory is such a glorious, triumphant word. I cannot use it in speaking of warfare that is illegal to many of us. Marse Robert's [1] approval and commendation of this illegitimate mode is a source of surprise, for, like many of us, the dear old

[1] General Lee.

"Tyee" was reared and schooled in honorable warfare.

Well, as Trenholm said, only those who have enlisted for this whole war, with muskets on their shoulders and knapsacks on their backs, have a right to criticize; but I reserve even from these the right, and acknowledge myself wrong in criticizing. An old army story, though hardly illustrative enough to be justifiable in telling, occurs to me:

An old major of artillery, who was always deploring the fact that he couldn't use his own favorite arm against the Indians, determined one day to try the *moral* effect of it upon a tribe of friendly ones nearby. So he took one of the small howitzers which defended the fort and securely strapped it to the back of an army mule, with the muzzle projecting over the mule's tail, and then proceeded with the captain, sergeant and orderly to the bluff on the bank of the Missouri where the Indians were encamped. The gun was loaded and primed, the fuse inserted and the mule backed to the very edge of the bluff.

The mule with his wonted curiosity, hearing the fizzing, turned his head to see what unusual thing was happening to him. The next second his feet were bunched up together, making forty revolutions a minute, the gun threatening with instant destruction everything within a radius of five miles. The captain climbed a tree, the sergeant and orderly following suit. The fat major, too heavy to climb, rolled over on the ground, alternately praying to God and cursing the mule. When the explosion came, the recoil of the gun and the wild leap of the terrified mule carried both over the bluff and to the bottom of the river. The captain, the sergeant and the poor, crestfallen, discomfited major, with the mule and the gun to account for, returned to the fort, soon to be waited on by the Indian chiefs, who had held a hurried council. The high chief, bowing his head up and down, said:

"Injun go home. Injun ver' brave. Injun love white man. Injun help white man. Injun heap use gun, use knife, heap use bow-arrow; but when white man shoot off whole jackass, Injun no think right—no can understand. Injun no help white man fight that way. Injun go home."

44

THE HEART OF A SOLDIER

So, my Sally, if you will forgive your Soldier for telling this old-time story and let him say that he does not approve of fighting in the way in which —— fights, he will bid you good-by and eat his breakfast, which the cook says is getting cold. Will you come, my darling, and have some coffee with your Soldier? It is some we captured, and is *real* coffee.

Come! The tin cup is clean and shining; but the corn-bread is greasy and smoked. And the bacon—that is greasy, too, but it is good and tastes all right, if it will only hold out till our Stars and Bars wave over the land of the free and the home of the brave, and we have our own home. Nevermore we'll hear of wars, but only love and life with its eternal joys.

YOUR OWN SOLDIER.

Headquarters, May —, 1862.

IV

In Which Are Given Certain Important Details of the Battle of Seven Pines

A VIOLENT storm was raging, flooding the level ground, as I wrote you last, followed the next day by one of fire and blood —the Battle of Seven Pines.

I pray that you accepted the invitation of your mountain chum, and that your beautiful eyes and tender heart have been spared the horrors of war which this battle must have poured into sad Richmond. Three hundred and fifty of your Soldier's brigade, 1,700 strong, were killed or wounded, and all fought as Virginians should, fighting as they did for the right, for love, honor, home and state— principles which they had been taught from the mothers' knees, the schoolroom and the pulpit.

Under orders from Old Peter,[1] we marched

[1] General Longstreet.

at daylight and reported to D. H. Hill, near
Seven Pines. Hill directed me to ride over
and communicate with Hood. I started at
once with Charlie and Archer, of my staff, to
obey this order, but had gone only a short distance when we met a part of the Louisiana
Zouaves in panic. I managed to seize and de-
tain one fellow, mounted on a mule that
seemed to have imbibed his rider's fear and
haste. The man dropped his plunder and
seizing his carbine threatened to kill me unless I released him at once, saying that the
Yankees were upon his heels. We galloped
back to Hill's headquarters—Archer bringing
up the rear with the Zouave, who explained
that the enemy were advancing in force and
were within a few hundred yards of us. Hill
ordered me to attack at once, which I did,
driving them through an abatis over a cross-
road leading to the railroad.

As we were nearing the second abatis, I, on
foot at the time, noticed that Armistead's Brigade had broken, and sent a courier back post-
haste to Hill for troops. A second and third
message were sent and then a fourth, telling
him that if he would send me more troops and

ammunition we could drive the enemy across the Chickahominy. But alas, Hill, as brave, as great, as heroic a soldier as he is, has, since the fall of Johnston, been so bothered and annoyed with countermanding orders that he was, if I may say so, confused and failed to respond. After this delay nothing was left for us but to withdraw. Hill sent two regiments of Colston's Brigade and ordered Mahone's Brigade on my right, and at one o'clock at night, under his orders, we withdrew in perfect order and the enemy retreated to their bosky cover.

Thus, my darling, was ended the Battle of Seven Pines. No shot was fired afterward. How I wish I could say it ended all battles and that the last shot that will ever be heard was fired on June first, 1862. What a change love does make! How tender all things become to a heart touched by love—how beautiful the beautiful is and how abhorrent is evil! See, my darling, see what power you have—guard it well.

I have heard that my dear old friend, McClellan, is lying ill about ten miles from here. May some loving, soothing hand minister to

"The enemy is there, General,
and I am going to strike him,"
said Marse Robert in his firm,
quiet voice.—Page 94.

him. He was, he is and he will always be,
even were his pistol pointed at my heart, my
dear, loved friend. May God bless him and
spare his life. You, my darling, may not be
in sympathy with this feeling, for I know you
see "no good in Nazareth." Forgive me for
feeling differently from you, little one, and
please don't love me any the less. You cannot
understand the *entente cordiale* between us
"old fellows."

Faithfully,

YOUR SOLDIER.

Mechanicsville Turnpike, June 1, 1862.

V

Containing a Presentiment of Danger—the Night Before He was Wounded at Gaines's Mill

ALL last night, my darling Sally, the spirit of my dear mother seemed to hover over me. When she was living and I used to feel in that way, I always, as sure as fate, received from her a letter written at the very time that I had the sensation of her presence. I wonder if up there she is watching over me, trying to send me some message—some warning. I wish I knew.

This morning my brigade moved from its cantonments on the Williamsburg road and by daybreak was marching along the Mechanicsville turnpike, leading north of Richmond. The destination and character of the expedition, my darling, is unknown; but the position of other troops indicates a general movement. This evening we crossed the Chickahominy and are bivouacked on our guns in the road in front of Mechanicsville, from which point

THE HEART OF A SOLDIER

I am blessing my spirit and refreshing my soul by sending a message to my promised wife. I am tired and sleepy, several times to-day going to sleep on my horse.

This war was really never contemplated in earnest. I believe if either the North or the South had expected that their differences would result in this obstinate struggle, the cold-blooded Puritan and the cock hatted Huguenot and Cavalier would have made a compromise. Poor old Virginia came oftener than Noah's dove with her olive branch. Though she desired to be loyal to the Union of States, she did not believe in the right of coercion, and when called upon to furnish troops to restrain her sister states she refused, and would not even permit the passage of an armed force through her domain for that purpose. With no thought of cost, she rolled up her sleeves, ready to risk all in defense of a principle consecrated by the blood of her fathers. And now, alas, it is too late. We must carry through this bitter task unto the end. May the end be soon!

YOUR SOLDIER.

In Camp, June 27, 1862.

VI

At His Old Home Recovering From His Wound

IT is only when you are here with me, my
darling, that I am not chafing, fretting,
under my enforced absence from my command. As poor a marksman as the Yankee
was who shot me, I wish he had been poorer
still, aiming, as he must have been, either at
my head or my heart and breaking my wing.
He was frightened, too, I suspect, and had,
besides, too much powder in his load. What
did you want with that shot-smoked, burnt
coat sleeve? The arm it held is yours to work
for and shield you, my love, for always.

Impatient and restive as I am to get back
to the field, letters and reports just received
show me that I am not missed and that my
gallant old brigade is proving its valor as
loyally under its new leader as when it so fearlessly followed your Soldier. It held Water-

loo Bridge against Pope while Jackson crossed the Rappahannock, and on the afternoon of the 30th received and repelled the on-set of Fitz John Porter, magnificently clearing the field and winning a victory for our arms.

The news came, too, this morning of the death of Kearny, one of the most brilliant generals of the Federal Army, a man whose fame as a soldier is world-wide. I knew him first in Mexico, where, as you know, he lost an arm at the siege of Mexico City. In Algeria he won the Cross of the Legion of Honor. He fought with the French in the battles of Magenta and Solferino and received also from Napoleon Third the decoration of the Legion of Honor. I wish we had taken him prisoner instead of shooting him. I hate to have such a man as Kearny killed. Marse Robert, who was his old friend, sent his body to Pope under a flag of truce. I am glad he did that—poor old Kearny!

The same courier, brought the sad news that our Ewell had lost a leg and our Talliaferro had been wounded. And these are the horrors to which, when away from you, my beautiful darling, your soldier is impatient to return.

Never, never did men, since the world began, fight like ours. The Duke of Somerset, who sneeringly laughed when he saw our ragged, dirty, barefooted soldiers—"Mostly beardless boys," as he said—took off his hat in reverence when he saw them fight.

Lovingly,
YOUR SOLDIER.

July 15, 1862.

VII

Mostly Concerning Bob, His Body-Servant

HOW I shall miss your visit to-day, my darling! I wish you had not gone. Don't stay. Doctor Minnegerode asked me this morning when he called, "Who sent the beautiful flowers?" Bob, to save me from answering, said, "De same young lady sont de flowers, Marse Doctor, dat 'broidered dat cape fer Marse George, en 'broidered dem dar slippers he's got on, en sont him de 'broidered stars dat he w'ars on his coat when he w'ars it; but *dat* young lady ain't de *onlyest* young lady dat sends Marse George flowers en things. No, Suh."

The dear old doctor understood; he winked at me and changed the subject. He is as loyal to the South, dear old fellow, as if his ancestors had landed at Jamestown. When he asked after my wound he said he would like to pray with me, though the dear old man

pronounced it, with his German accent,
"bray," and that reminded me of a story, and
instead of having my thoughts and my heart
set upon his beautiful prayer as I should have
—miserable sinner that I was—I began thinking of Tom August, who said that one Sunday
someone meeting him coming out of Old St.
Paul's asked him what was the matter. He
replied, "Oh, nothing. I'm not a jackass and
I'm not going to bray, and old Doctor Minnegerode not only insists that I, but that his
whole congregation, shall 'bray.' I, for one,
will not do it and I don't want to make a row
about it; so I came out. I wonder what the
effect would be if we took him literally and
did all 'bray'?"

Now, my darling, forgive this foolish story.
I learned to like story-telling, listening as a
boy to the best story-teller in the world, Mr.
Lincoln.

Even the bird knows you are not coming
to-day, for he doesn't sing. I shall hold you
to the last line of your sweet note, which says,
"I'll come to you, my Soldier, before the
flowers die." When Bob asked me, "Is Miss
Sallie comin' dis ebenin' er in de mornin'?"

I answered, "She does not mention any set time, Bob. She only says she'll come before the flowers die." "De flowers ain't waxinated flowers, is dey, Marse George?" he asked. "Den if dey ain't waxinated 'twon't be long fo' she is here."

When I asked him to hold the paper while I wrote, he humbly, beseechingly asked, "Please, Suh, Marse George, ef hit ain't axin' too much, when you comes ter writin' er dem dar words lak love en honey en darlin', er any er dem poetry rhymes 'bout roses red en violets blue, won't you please, Suh, show 'em ter me?" I didn't promise him, my sweetheart. I only said, "Hold that paper steady, Sir, and don't let it slip." But when I did call you "darling" or tell you I loved you, I felt so guilty that the rascal knew it and grinned.

Your own
SOLDIER.

July 18, 1862.

VIII

Written Upon His Return to His Old Command

DARLING, my heart turns to you with a love so great that pain follows in its wake. You cannot understand this, my beautiful, bright-eyed, sunny-hearted princess. Your face, is the sweetest face in all the world, mirroring, as it does, all that is pure and unselfish, and I must not cast a shadow over it by the fears that come to me, in spite of myself. No, a soldier should not know fear of any kind. I must fight and plan and hope, and you must pray. Pray for a realization of all our beautiful dreams, sitting beside our own hearthstone in our own home—you and I, you my goddess of devotion, and I your devoted slave. May God in his mercy spare my life and make it worthy of you!

My shoulder and arm are still quite stiff, and I cannot yet put my sleeve on the wounded arm. I have on one sleeve, and my coat is thrown over my other shoulder and other arm.

I can reach my mouth with my hand by bending my neck way over; so I am not helpless. Bob still buttons my collar and does some other little services. Until I have more control of my arm, however, I shall confine myself to riding old Black and not venture on Lucy. Enough of so small a matter.

My boys are delighted to welcome me back, showing their affection for me in many, many ways. Garnett is still in command of my dear old brigade, which was temporarily turned over to him when I was wounded and which, under his gallant leadership, has sustained its old reputation for fearlessness and endurance. I miss dear, familiar faces, for many of the brave fellows have been killed and wounded. You have heard me speak of Colonel Strange —a gallant soldier. He was wounded and left behind. After he was shot the plucky old chap called out in a loud, clear voice, "Stand firm, boys; stand firm."

Well, the Yankees won the battle, but McClellan's delay in winning enabled Old Jack [1] to seize Harper's Ferry, so it was not so great a victory for them after all. Old Jack's note

[1] General Stonewall Jackson.

to Marse Robert, telling him of his success, was characteristic in both brevity and diction. He said, "Through God's mercy Harper's Ferry and its garrison are *to be* surrendered."

The seventeenth following is recorded in letters of blood for both armies, and in its wake came Lincoln's great political victory, proving the might of the pen, in his Emancipation Proclamation—winning with it the greatest victory yet for the North. It will behoove us now to heed well the old story of "The Lark and the Husbandman," for it will be farewell to all foreign intervention unless Greek meets Greek and we fight fire with fire and we, too, issue an Emancipation Proclamation. I pray God that the powers that reign will have the wisdom and foresight to see this in its true and all-pervading light. It would end the war, and I should assume as soon as practicable the rôle of schoolmaster and husband to the brightest little pupil and the sweetest little wife in all the world.

YOUR SOLDIER.

P. S. Have been placed temporarily in command of a division.

Headquarters, Sept. 25, 1862.

IX

On the Occasion of His Promotion to the Rank of Major-General—Telling of Jackson and Garnett

TO-DAY I was officially promoted to the rank of Major-General and permanently placed in command of a division. My dear old brigade, which I love and which was with me in the battles of Williamsburg, Seven Pines and Gaines's Mill, was assigned to General Garnett and there comes somehow, in spite of everything, a little "kind of curious" feeling within when I hear it called "Garnett's Brigade," even though he has been in command of it almost ever since I was wounded and has won for it distinction and from it love and respect.

Old Dick is a fine fellow, a brave, splendid soldier. He was in the Mexican war and was wounded in the battle of Mexico. He commanded a brigade under Old Jack and was for a time in command of the famous old "Stonewall Brigade." You have not met him, my sweetheart; but I want you to know him. He is as sensitive and proud as he is fearless and sweet-spirited, and has felt more keenly than most men would Old Jack's censure of him at the battle of Kernstown, when all his ammunition gave out and he withdrew his brigade from the field, for which Old Jack had him arrested and relieved from duty. Old Jack told Lawton that in arresting Garnett he had no reference to his want of daring, which was surprising for Old Jack to say, who never explains anything.

Lawton, who is one of his generals, says Old Jack holds himself as the god of war, giving short, sharp commands, distinctly, rapidly and decisively, without consultation or explanation and disregarding suggestions and remonstrances. Being himself absolutely fearless, and having unusual mental and moral, as well as physical, courage, he goes ahead on his own hook, asking no advice and resenting interference. He places no value on human life, caring for nothing so much as fighting, unless it be praying. Illness, wounds and all disabilities he defines as inefficiency and indications of a lack of patriotism. Suffering from insomnia, he often uses his men as a sedative, and when he can't sleep calls them out, marches them out a few miles; then marches them back. He never praises his men for gallantry, because it is their duty to be gallant and they do not deserve credit for doing their duty. Well, my own darling, I only pray that God may spare him to us to see us through. If General Lee had Grant's resources he would soon end the war; but Old Jack can do it without resources.

Bless your heart, here I am talking of these old war-horses to my flower queen. Well, she knows how entirely I love her and how I have left in her keeping my soul's all.

Lovingly and faithfully,

YOUR SOLDIER.

Headquarters, Oct. 11, 1862.

X

From the Field of Fredericksburg

HERE we are, my darling, at Fredericksburg, on the south side of the Rappahannock, half-way between Richmond and Washington, fortified for us by the hand of the Great Father.

I penciled you a note by old Jackerie [1] on the 12th from the foot of the Hills between Hazel Run and the Telegraph Road. In it I sent a hyacinth—given me by a pretty lady who came out with beaten biscuit—and some unwritten and written messages from Old Peter and Old Jack, Hood, Ewell, Stuart, and your "brothers," to the "someone" to whom I was writing.

My division, nine thousand strong, is in fine shape. It was on the field of battle, as a division, for the first time yesterday, though only one brigade, Kemper's, was actively engaged.

[1] Headquarters Postmaster.

What a day it was, my darling—this ever to be remembered by many of us thirteenth of December—dawning auspiciously upon us clad in deepest, darkest mourning! A fog such as would shame London lay over the valley, and through the dense mist *distinctly* came the uncanny commands of the unseen opposing officers. My men were eager to be in the midst of the fight, and if Hood had not been so cautious they would probably have immortalized themselves. Old Peter's orders were that Hood and myself were to hold our ground of defense unless we should see an opportunity to attack the enemy while engaged with A. P. Hill on the right. A little after ten, when the fog had lifted and Stuart's cannon from the plain of Massaponax were turned upon Meade and when Franklin's advance left the enemy's flank open, I went up to Hood and urged him to seize the opportunity; but he was afraid to assume so great a responsibility and sent for permission to Old Peter, who was with Marse Robert in a different part of the field. Before his assent and approval were received, the opportunity, alas, was lost!

If war, my darling, is a necessity—and I

suppose it is—it is a very cruel one. Your Soldier's heart almost stood still as he watched those sons of Erin fearlessly rush to their death. The brilliant assault on Marye's Heights of their Irish Brigade was beyond description. Why, my darling, we forgot they were fighting us, and cheer after cheer at their fearlessness went up all along our lines. About fifty of my division sleep their last sleep at the foot of Marye's Heights.

I can't help feeling sorry for Old Burnside —proud, plucky, hard-headed old dog. I always liked him, but I loved little Mac,[1] and it was a godsend to the Confederacy that he was relieved.

Oh, my darling, war and its results did not seem so awful till the love for you came. Now—now I want to love and bless and help everything, and there are no foes—no enemies —just love for you and longing for you.

YOUR SOLDIER.

Fredericksburg, Dec. 14, 1862.

[1] General McClellan.

PART TWO

During the Six Months
Campaign Before
Gettysburg

*D*URING the period covered by the letters in this part the burdens of the war fell heavily upon the soul of the General's little sweetheart, as they did upon the whole South. Lee's campaign into Pennsylvania carried his army for many months into the country of the enemy. It was a land that was strange to the men and stranger still to the imagination of the sorrowing ones who stayed behind. And at the end of it came Gettysburg, where more than five thousand sons and husbands and lovers laid down their lives for the cause they thought to be just.

Pickett's charge at Gettysburg is one of those deeds of arms that are immortal. When it was over—ending in defeat as it did, on account of the lack of promised supports—two-thirds of his beloved division lay sleeping on the slope of Cemetary Ridge and the heart of their fearless commander was crushed by the thought of their sacrifice and the suffering that it meant to the Southland.

XI

*From the General's Old Home On the Suffolk
Expedition*

TO-DAY I rode on ahead of my division,
stopped for a moment at our old home,
ran into the garden and gathered for my darling some lilies of the valley, planted by my
sweet mother, which I knew were now in the
full glory of their blossoming. As I plucked
them one by one, I thought of the dear mother
who had planted them and the sweet bride-
to-be who would receive them, and my heart
went up in gratitude for the great love given
me by both.

While I am writing to you, Braxton and
the cook and the whole household, in fact,
are busy getting a lunch for me and preparing
to load up my courier and my boy, Bob, with
as many more lunches as they can carry, to be
distributed as far as they will go. My little
sister is making a paper box to hold my lilies

for you, and I am writing a love-letter to stand sentinel over them and guard the sweet, sacred messages entrusted to them. Old Jackerie will take them to you and will also bring you, with my sister's love, a box of her own home-made dulces.

Perhaps, sweetheart, *perhaps* I say, you will see your Soldier sooner than you think. You know that since the capture of Roanoke Island and our abandonment of Norfolk and Suffolk, all that section of the country has been in the hands of the enemy. Now in the extreme northeast corner of North Carolina are stored away large quantities of corn and bacon. Old Peter, our far-seeing, slow but sure, indefatigable, plodding old war-horse, has planned to secure some of these sorely needed supplies for our poor, half fed army—and there never was such an army, such an uncomplaining, plucky body of men—never.

Why, my darling, during these continuous ten days' march, the ground snowy and sleety, the feet of many of these soldiers covered only with improvised moccasins of raw beef hide, and hundreds of them without shoes or blankets or overcoats, they have not uttered one word of complaint, nor one murmuring tone; but cheerily, singing or telling stories, they have tramped — tramped — tramped. To crown it all, after having marched sixty miles over half frozen, slushy roads they passed to-day through Richmond, the home of many of them, without a halt, with not a straggler— greeted and cheered by sweethearts, wives, mothers and friends. "God bless you, my darling," "God bless you, my son," "Hello, old man," "Howdy, Charley," rang all along the line. Lunches, slices of bread and meat, bottles of milk or hot coffee were thrust into grateful hands by the dear people of Richmond, who thus brought comfort and cheer to many a hungry one besides their very own, as the men hurriedly returned the greetings and marched on. You would hardly recognize these ragged, barefoot soldiers as the trim, tidy boys of two years ago in their handsome gray uniforms, with shining equipment and full haversacks and knapsacks.

Be brave and help me to be brave, my darling, and to trust in God. I won't say, "Keep your powder dry," for one who doesn't know enough to do that is not much of a soldier.

Faithfully and forever your

SOLDIER.

Richmond, February, 1863.

XII

In Which He Urges his Betrothed to Marry Him at Once

THIS morning I awakened from a beautiful dream, and while its glory still overshadows the waking and fills my soul with radiance I write to make an earnest request—entreating, praying, that you will grant it. You know, my darling, we have no prophets in these days to tell us how near or how far is the end of this awful struggle. If "the battle is not to the strong" then we may win; but when all our ports are closed and the world is against us, when for us a man killed is a man lost, while Grant may have twenty-five of every nation to replace one of his, it seems that the battle is to the strong. So often already has hope been dashed to the winds.

Why, dear, only a little while since, the Army of the Potomac recrossed the Rappahannock, defeated, broken in spirit, the men deserting, the subordinate officers so severe in their criticism of their superiors that the great Commander-in-Chief of the Army, Mr. Lincoln, felt it incumbent upon him to write a severe letter of censure and rebuke. Note the change and hear their bugle-call of hope. Hooker, who is alleged to have "the finest army on the planet," is reported to be on the eve of moving against Richmond. My division and that of Hood, together with the artillery of Dearing and Henry, have been ordered to a point near Petersburg to meet this possible movement.

Now, my darling, may angels guide my pen and help me to write—help me to voice this longing desire of my heart and intercede for me with you for a speedy fulfillment of your promise to be my wife. As you know, it is imperative that I should remain at my post and absolutely impossible for me to come for you. So you will have to come to me. Will you, dear? Will you come? Can't your beautiful eyes see beyond the mist of my eagerness and anxiety that in the bewilderment of my worship—worshiping, as I do, one so divinely right, and feeling that my love is re-

74

turned—how hard it is for me to ask you to overlook old-time customs, remembering only that you are to be a soldier's wife? A week, a day, an hour as your husband would engulf in its great joy all my past woes and ameliorate all future fears.

So, my Sally, don't let's wait; send me a line back by Jackerie saying you will come. Come at once, my darling, into this valley of the shadow of uncertainty, and make certain the comfort that if I should fall I shall fall as your husband.

You know that I love you with a devotion that absorbs all else—a devotion so divine that when in dreams I see you it is as something too pure and sacred for mortal touch. And if you only knew the heavenly life which thrills me through when I make it real to myself that you love me, you would understand. Think, my dear little one, of the uncertainty and dangers of even a day of separation, and don't let the time come when either of us will look back and say, "It might have been."

If I am spared, my dear, all my life shall be devoted to making you happy, to keeping all that would hurt you far from you, to making

75

all that is good come near to you. Heaven
will help me to be ever helpful to you and
will bless me to bless you. If you knew how
every hour I kneel at your altar, if you could
hear the prayers I offer to you and to our
Heavenly Father for you, if you knew the incessant thought and longing and desire to
make you blessed, you would know how much
your answer will mean to me and how, while
I plead, I am held back by a reverence and a
sensitive adoration for you. For, my Sally,
you are my goddess and I am only

Your devoted,

SOLDIER.

In Camp, April 15, 1863.

NOTE: To those who recall the rigid system of social
training in which a girl of that period was reared, it will
not seem strange that a maiden, even in war times, could
not seriously contemplate the possibility of leaving home
and being married by the wayside in that desultory and
unstudied fashion. So, though my heart responded to
the call, what could I do but adhere to the social laws,
more formidable than were ever the majestic canons of
the ecclesiasts? My Soldier admitted that I was right,
and we agreed to await a more favorable time.—LA-
SALLE CORBELL PICKETT.

XIII

Warning Her to Leave the Danger Zone

HOPING, my darling, that you heeded your Soldier's admonition, and are now safe across the "Black Water," I am taking the risk of sending to you at Ivor, by my boy servant, Bob, a little box of dulces and a note filled with adoration.

My orders to follow Hood's Division have been countermanded. Hood was hurried on from the "Black Water" by rail to rejoin Marse Robert, who has just gained a great victory at Chancellorsville. I am ordered instead to proceed *at once* with three of my brigades to Petersburg, via the "Jerusalem-Plank-Road," to intercept a cavalry raid.

Perhaps, my darling, I shall have met these raiders ere this reaches you. Who knows how many of us may then hear the roll-call from the other side and be sorry? But sorry for whom? For the comrades who answer to their names and are reported present, or for those whose spirit voices, just born, have not yet gained the power to reach the ear of the orderly and who are reported dead, even though they, too, answer, "Here"? For, my darling, *there is no death,* and you must feel —must *know*—now and always, that whether here or there, at the roll-call your Soldier answers, *"Here."*

Now, adieu, my beloved. Close your brown eyes and feel my arms around you, for I am holding you close—oh, so close!

Forever your

SOLDIER.

Suffolk, May 5, 1863.

XIV

Written When Lee Crossed the Potomac

EACH day, my darling, takes me farther and farther away from you, from all I love and hold dear. We have been guarding the passes of the Blue Ridge. To-day, under orders from Marse Robert, we cross the Potomac. McLaws' and Hood's Divisions and the three brigades of my division follow on after Hill. May our Heavenly Father bless us with an early and a victorious return. But even then, the price of it—the price of it, my little one—the blood of our countrymen! God in His mercy temper the wind to us!

As I returned the salute of my men, many of them beardless boys, the terrible responsibility as their Commander almost overwhelmed me, and my heart was rent in prayer for guidance and help. Oh, the desolate homes—the widows and orphans and heartbroken mothers that this campaign will make! How many of them, so full of hope and cheer now, will cross that other river which lands them at the Eternal Home.

Have faith, my little one; keep up a "skookum tum-tum." [1] Your soldier feels that he will return to claim his bride—his beautiful, glorious bride. And then we shall be so happy, my darling, that all our days to come, we will show our loving gratitude to our Father for His mercy in sparing us to each other.

Now, my Sally, how I hate to say it—adieu. Do you remember how many times we said good-by that last evening? And then as I heard the latch of the gate click and shut me out, I was obliged to go back. I could not stand the cruelty of the sound of that latch—it seemed to knife my soul. I turned back and said, "Good night!" The door was open; I came in. You thought I had gone. I can't just remember how many times I said good night. I know I did not close the gate as I went out again. Keep another gate open for the good morning, my precious bride-to-be. Oh, the bliss to be—the bliss to be then for

YOUR SOLDIER.

In Camp, June 18, 1863.

[1] Chinook for strong heart.

XV

On the Way Through Pennsylvania

I NEVER could quite enjoy being a "Conquering Hero." No, my dear, there is something radically wrong about my Hurrahism. I can fight for a cause I know to be just, can risk my own life and the lives of those in my keeping without a thought of the consequences; but when we've conquered, when we've downed the enemy and won the victory, I don't want to hurrah. I want to go off all by myself and be sorry for them—want to lie down in the grass, away off in the woods somewhere or in some lone valley on the hillside far from all *human* sound, and rest my soul and put my heart to sleep and get back something—I don't know what—but something I had that is gone from me—something subtle and unexplainable—something I never knew I had till I had lost it—till it was gone—gone —gone!

Yesterday my men were marching victoriously through the little town of Greencastle, the bands all playing our glorious, soul inspiring, southern airs: "The Bonny Blue Flag," "My Maryland," "Her Bright Smile Haunts Me Still," and the soldiers all happy, hopeful, joyously keeping time to the music, many following it with their voices and making up for the want of the welcome they were not receiving in the enemy's country by cheering themselves and giving themselves a welcome. As Floweree's band, playing "Dixie," was passing a vine-bowered home, a young girl rushed out on the porch and waved a United States flag. Then, either fearing that it might be taken from her or finding it too large and unwieldy, she fastened it around her as an apron, and taking hold of it on each side and waving it in defiance, called out with all the strength of her girlish voice and all the courage of her brave young heart:

"Traitors—traitors—traitors, come and take this flag, the man of you who dares!"

Knowing that many of my men were from a section of the country which had been within the enemy's lines, and fearing lest some might forget their manhood, I took off my hat and bowed to her, saluted her flag and then turned, facing the men who felt and saw my unspoken order. And don't you know that they were all Virginians and didn't forget it, and that almost every man lifted his cap and cheered the little maiden who, though she kept on waving her flag, ceased calling us traitors, till letting it drop in front of her she cried out:

"Oh, I wish—I wish I had a rebel flag; I'd wave that, too."

The picture of that little girl in the vine-covered porch, beneath the purple morning glories with their closed lips and bowed heads waiting and saving their prettiness and bloom for the coming morn—of course, I thought of *you,* my darling. For the time, that little Greencastle Yankee girl with her beloved flag was my own little promised-to-be-wife, receiving from her Soldier and her Soldier's soldiers the reverence and homage due her.

We left the little girl standing there with the flag gathered up in her arms, as if too sacred to be waved now that even the enemy had done it reverence.   As ever,

YOUR SOLDIER.

Greencastle, Pa., June 24, 1863.
83

XVI

Lines Penned on the Road to Gettysburg

WE crossed the Potomac on the 24th at Williamsport and went into bivouac on the Maryland side, from which place I sent my Lady-Love a long letter and some flowers gathered on the way. We then went on to Hagerstown, where we met A. P. Hill's Corps, which had crossed the river farther down. From Hagerstown I sent to the same and only Lady-Love another letter, which was not only freighted with all the adoration and devotion of her Soldier's heart, but contained messages from the staff and promises to take care of him and bring him safely back to her.

We made no delay at Hagerstown, but passing through in the rear of Hill's Corps moved on up Cumberland Valley and bivouacked at Greencastle, where the most homesick letter of all yet written was sent to—well, guess *whom* this time. Why, to the same Lady-Love, the

84

sweetest, loveliest flower that ever blossomed to bless and make fairer a beautiful world—for it is beautiful, betokening in its loveliness nothing of this deadly strife between men who should be brethren of a great and common cause, as they are the heritage of a great and common country.

The officers and men are all in excellent condition, bright and cheerful, singing songs and telling stories, full of hope and courage, inspired with absolute faith and confidence in our success. There is no straggling, no disorder, no dissatisfaction, no plundering, and there are no desertions. Think of it, my darling—an army of sixty thousand men marching through the enemy's country without the *least* opposition! The object of this great movement is, of course, unknown to us. Its purpose and our destination are known at present only to the Commanding General and his Chief Lieutenants. The men generally believe that the intention is to entirely surround the Army of the Potomac and place Washington and Baltimore within our grasp. They think that Marse Robert is merely threatening the northern cities, with the view of suddenly turning down the Susquehanna, cutting off all railroad connections, destroying all bridges, throwing his army north of Baltimore and cutting off Washington, and that Beauregard is to follow on directly from Richmond via Manassas to Washington, in rear of Hooker, who of course will be in pursuit of Marse Robert.

Nous verrons.

We reached here this morning, June 27th, the anniversary of the battle of Gaines's Mill, where your Soldier was wounded. We marched straight through the town of Chambersburg, which was more deserted than Goldsmith's village. The stores and houses were all closed, with here and there groups of uncheerful Boers of Deutschland descent, earnestly talking, more sylvan shadows than smiles wreathing their faces. I had given orders that the bands were not to play; but as we were marching through the northeastern part of the city, some young ladies came out onto the veranda of one of the prettiest homes in the town and asked:

"Would you mind shooting off the bands a bit?"

THE HEART OF A SOLDIER

So the command was given and the band played "Home Sweet Home," "Annie Laurie," "Her Bright Smile Haunts Me Still," "Nellie Gray" and "Hazel Dell." The young ladies asked the next band that passed if they wouldn't play "Dixie"; but the band instead struck up "The Old Oaken Bucket," "The Swanee River," "The Old Arm Chair," "The Lone Rock by the Sea" and "Auld Lang Syne."

"Thought you was rebels. Where'd you come from anyhow? Can't play 'Dixie,' none of you," they called out. We marched straight on through the city and are camped four miles beyond the town on the York River road.

To-morrow, if you'll promise not to divulge it to a human soul, I'll tell you a great secret. No, my darling, I can't wait till to-morrow. I'll tell you right now. So listen and cross your heart that you won't tell. I love you— love you—love you, and oh, little one, I want to see you so! That is the secret.

Lovingly and forever,
YOUR SOLDIER.

Chambersburg, June 27, 1863.

XVII

During a Halt in the Long March

I WISH, my darling, you could see this wonderfully rich and prosperous country, abounding in plenty, with its great, strong, vigorous horses and oxen, its cows and crops and verdantly thriving vegetation—none of the ravages of war, no signs of devastation— all in woeful contrast to the land where we lay dreaming. All the time I break the law "Thou shalt not covet," for every fine horse or cow I see I want for my darling, and all the pretty things I see besides. Never mind, she shall have everything some day, and I shall have the universe and heaven's choicest gift when she is my wife—all my very own.

At Chambersburg, Marse Robert preached us a sermon, first instructing us in the meaning of "meum" and "teum," and then taking as his text, "Vengeance is Mine, saith the Lord." I observed that the mourners' bench was not overcrowded with seekers for conversion.

The poor fellows were thinking of their own despoiled homes, looted of everything, and were not wildly enthusiastic as they acquiesced obediently to our beloved Commander's order. The Yanks have taken into the mountains and across the Susquehanna all the supplies they could, and we pay liberally for those which we are compelled to take, paying for them in money which is paid to us, our own Confederate script. Some of us have a few pieces of gold with which to purchase some keepsake or token for the dear ones at home. Alas, my little one, how many of us will be blessed with the giving of them? God in His mercy be our Commander-in-Chief!

We have not a wide field for selection here, as we once had at Price's dry goods store or John Tyler's jewelry establishment in Richmond; but it seems quite magnificent to us now, since the Richmond counters are so bare as to offer not even a wedding ring or a yard of calico. We are guying General —— who, after long and grave deliberation, bought three hoop skirts as a present for his betrothed.

THE HEART OF A SOLDIER

All that makes life dear is the thought of seeing you and being with you. And oh, what an eternity it seems since I said good night! Oh, my darling, love me, pray for me, hold me in your thoughts, keep me in your heart!

Our whole army is now in Pennsylvania, north of the river. There were rumors that Richmond was threatened from all sides—Dix from Old Point, Getty from Hanover, Keyes from Bottom's Bridge, and so on—and that we might be recalled. It turned out to be Munchausen, and we are still to march forward. Every tramp—tramp—tramp is a thought—thought—thought of my darling, every halt a blessing invoked, every command a loving caress; and the thought of you and prayer for you make me strong, make me better, give me courage, give me faith. Now, my dearest, let my soul speak to yours. Listen—listen—listen! You hear—I am answered.

Forever and ever,

YOUR SOLDIER.

In Camp, June 29, 1863.

XVIII

Written While He Awaited the Order to Charge at Gettysburg

CAN my prettice do patchwork? If she can, she must piece together these penciled scraps of soiled paper and make out of them, not a log-cabin quilt, but a wren's nest, cement it with love and fill it with blue and golden and speckled eggs of faith and hope, to hatch out greater love yet for us.

Well, the long, wearying march from Chambersburg, through dust and heat beyond compare, brought us here yesterday (a few miles from Gettysburg). Though my poor men were almost exhausted by the march in the intense heat, I felt that the exigencies demanded my assuring Marse Robert that we had arrived and that, with a few hours' rest, my men would be equal to anything he might require of them. I sent Walter with my message and rode on myself to Little Round Top to see Old Peter, who, I tell you, dearest, was mighty glad to see me. And now, just think of it, though the old war-horse was watching A. P. Hill's attack upon the center and Hood and McLaws of his own corps, who had struck Sickles, he turned and before referring to the fighting or asking about the march inquired after *you,* my darling! While we were watching the fight Walter came back with Marse Robert's reply to my message, which was in part: "Tell Pickett I'm glad that he has come, that I can always depend upon him and his men, but that I shall not want him this evening."

We have been on the *qui vive,* sweetheart, since midnight and as early as three o'clock were on the march. About half past three, Gary's pistol signaled the Yankees' attack upon Culp's Hill, and with its echo a wail of regret went up from my very soul that the other two brigades of my old division had been left behind. Oh, God, if only I had them—a surety for the honor of Virginia, for I can depend upon them, little one. They know your Soldier and would follow him into the very jaws of death—and he will need them, right here, too, before he's through.

At early dawn, darkened by the threatening rain, Armistead, Garnett, Kemper and your Soldier held a heart-to-heart powwow.

All three sent regards to you, and Old Lewis pulled a ring from his little finger and making me take it, said, "Give this little token, George, please, to her of the sunset eyes, with my love, and tell her the 'old man' says since he could not be the lucky dog he's mighty glad that you are."

Dear old Lewis—dear old "Lo," as Magruder always called him, being short for Lothario. Well, my Sally, I'll keep the ring for you, and some day I'll take it to John Tyler and have it made into a breastpin and set around with rubies and diamonds and emeralds. You will be the pearl, the other jewel. Dear old Lewis!

Just as we three separated to go our different ways after silently clasping hands, our fears and prayers voiced in the "Good luck, old man," a summons came from Old Peter, and I immediately rode to the top of the ridge where he and Marse Robert were making a reconnaissance of Meade's position. "Great God!" said Old Peter as I came up. "Look, General Lee, at the insurmountable difficulties between our line and that of the Yankees —the steep hills, the tiers of artillery, the fences, the heavy skirmish line—and then we'll have to fight our infantry against their batteries. Look at the ground we'll have to charge over, nearly a mile of that open ground there under the rain of their canister and shrapnel."

"The enemy is there, General Longstreet, and I am going to strike him," said Marse Robert in his firm, quiet, determined voice.

About 8 o'clock I rode with them along our line of prostrate infantry. They had been told to lie down to prevent attracting attention, and though they had been forbidden to cheer they voluntarily arose and lifted in reverential adoration their caps to our beloved commander as we rode slowly along.

94

THE HEART OF A SOLDIER

Oh, the responsibility for the lives of such men as these! Well, my darling, their fate and that of our beloved Southland will be settled ere your glorious brown eyes rest on these scraps of penciled paper—your Soldier's last letter, perhaps.

Our line of battle faces Cemetery Ridge. Our detachments have been thrown forward to support our artillery which stretches over a mile along the crests of Oak Ridge and Seminary Ridge. The men are lying in the rear, my darling, and the hot July sun pours its scorching rays almost vertically down upon them. The suffering and waiting are almost unbearable.

.   .   .   .

Well, my sweetheart, at one o'clock the awful silence was broken by a cannon-shot and then another, and then more than a hundred guns shook the hills from crest to base, answered by more than another hundred—the whole world a blazing volcano, the whole of heaven a thunderbolt—then darkness and absolute silence—then the grim and gruesome, low-spoken commands—then the forming of

95

the attacking columns. My brave Virginians are to attack in front. Oh, may God in mercy help me as He never helped before!

I have ridden up to report to Old Peter. I shall give him this letter to mail to you and a package to give you if— Oh, my darling, do you feel the love of my heart, the prayer, as I write that fatal word?

Now, I go; but remember always that I love you with all my heart and soul, with every fiber of my being; that now and forever I am yours—yours, my beloved. It is almost three o'clock. My soul reaches out to yours—my prayers. I'll keep up a skookum tumtum for Virginia and for you, my darling.

YOUR SOLDIER.

Gettysburg, July 3, 1863.

XIX

Relating Certain Incidents of the Great Battle

MY letter of yesterday, my darling, written before the battle, was full of hope and cheer; even though it told you of the long hours of waiting from four in the morning, when Gary's pistol rang out from the Federal lines signaling the attack upon Culp's Hill, to the solemn eight-o'clock review of my men, who rose and stood silently lifting their hats in loving reverence as Marse Robert, Old Peter and your own Soldier reviewed them— on then to the deadly stillness of the five hours following, when the men lay in the tall grass in the rear of the artillery line, the July sun pouring its scorching rays almost vertically down upon them, till one o'clock when the awful silence of the vast battlefield was broken by a cannon-shot which opened the greatest artillery duel of the world. The firing lasted two hours. When it ceased we took advantage of the blackened field and in the glowering darkness formed our attacking column just before the brow of Seminary Ridge.

I closed my letter to you a little before three o'clock and rode up to Old Peter for orders. I found him like a great lion at bay. I have never seen him so grave and troubled. For several minutes after I had saluted him he looked at me without speaking. Then in an agonized voice, the reserve all gone, he said:

"Pickett, I am being crucified at the thought of the sacrifice of life which this attack will make. I have instructed Alexander to watch the effect of our fire upon the enemy, and when it begins to tell he must take the responsibility and give you your orders, for I can't."

While he was yet speaking a note was brought to me from Alexander. After reading it I handed it to him, asking if I should obey and go forward. He looked at me for a moment, then held out his hand. Presently, clasping his other hand over mine without speaking he bowed his head upon his breast. I shall never forget the look in his face nor the clasp of his hand when I said:—"Then, General, I shall lead my Division on." I had ridden only a few paces when I remembered your letter and (forgive me) thoughtlessly scribbled in a corner of the envelope, "If Old Peter's nod means death then good-by and God bless you, little one," turned back and asked the dear old chief if he would be good enough to mail it for me. As he took your letter from me, my darling, I saw tears glistening on his cheeks and beard. The stern old war-horse, God bless him, was weeping for his men and, I know, praying too that this cup might pass from them. I obeyed the silent assent of his bowed head, an assent given against his own convictions,—given in anguish and with reluctance.

My brave boys were full of hope and confident of victory as I led them forth, forming them in column of attack, and though officers and men alike knew what was before them,— knew the odds against them,—they eagerly offered up their lives on the altar of duty, having absolute faith in their ultimate success.

THE HEART OF A SOLDIER

Over on Cemetery Ridge the Federals beheld a scene never before witnessed on this continent,—a scene which has never previously been enacted and can never take place again—an army forming in line of battle in full view, under their very eyes—charging across a space nearly a mile in length over fields of waving grain and anon of stubble and then a smooth expanse—moving with the steadiness of a dress parade, the pride and glory soon to be crushed by an overwhelming heartbreak.[1]

. . . .

Well, it is all over now. The battle is lost, and many of us are prisoners, many are dead, many wounded, bleeding and dying. Your Soldier lives and mourns and but for you, my darling, he would rather, a million times rather, be back there with his dead, to sleep for all time in an unknown grave.

Your sorrowing
SOLDIER.

In Camp, July 4, 1863.

[1] Here follows a detailed account of the battle, which is omitted from this volume for the reasons given in the note on page 211.

XX

*Written in Sorrow and Defeat, Three Days
After the Struggle*

ON the Fourth—far from a glorious
Fourth to us or to any with love for his
fellow-men—I wrote you just a line of heartbreak. The sacrifice of life on that blood-
soaked field on the fatal third was too awful
for the heralding of victory, even for our victorious foe, who I think, believe as we do, that
it decided the fate of our cause. No words
can picture the anguish of that roll-call—the
breathless waits between the responses. The
"Here" of those who, by God's mercy, had
miraculously escaped the awful rain of shot
and shell was a sob—a gasp—a knell—for the
unanswered name of his comrade. There was
no tone of thankfulness for having been
spared to answer to their names, but rather a
toll, and an unvoiced wish that they, too, had
been among the missing.

THE HEART OF A SOLDIER

Even now I can hear them cheering as I gave the order, "Forward!" I can feel the thrill of their joyous voices as they called out all along the line, "We'll follow you, Marse George. We'll follow you—we'll follow you." Oh, how faithfully they kept their word—following me on—on—to their death, and I, believing in the promised support, led them on—on—on— Oh, God!

I can't write you a love-letter to-day, my Sally, for with my great love for you and my gratitude to God for sparing my life to devote to you, comes the overpowering thought of those whose lives were sacrificed—of the broken-hearted widows and mothers and orphans. The moans of my wounded boys, the sight of the dead, upturned faces, flood my soul with grief—and here am I whom they trusted, whom they followed, leaving them on that field of carnage—and guarding four thousand prisoners across the river back to Winchester. Such a duty for men who a few hours ago covered themselves with glory eternal!

Well, my darling, I put the prisoners all on their honor and gave them equal liberties with my own soldier boys. My first command to them was to go and enjoy themselves the best they could, and they have obeyed my order. To-day a Dutchman and two of his comrades came up and told me that they were lost and besought me to help them find their comrades. They had been with my men and were separated from their own comrades. So I sent old Floyd off on St. Paul to find out where they belonged and deliver them.

This is too gloomy and too poor a letter for so beautiful a sweetheart, but it seems sacrilegious, almost, to say I love you, with the hearts that are stilled to love on the field of battle.

YOUR SOLDIER.

Headquarters, July 6, 1863.

XXI

Containing Further Details of the Battle

I AM enclosing you a copy of General Lee's official letter of July 9th, in answer to mine of the 8th, the same day on which I wrote you (who deserved something brighter) that ghostly, woeful letter.

General Lee's letter has been published to the division in general orders and received with appreciative satisfaction. The soldiers, one and all, love and honor Lee, and his sympathy and praise are always very dear to them. Just after the order was published I heard one of the men, rather rough and uncouth and not, as are most of the men, to the manner born, say, as he wiped away the tears with the back of his hand, "Dag-gone him, dag-gone him, dag-gone his old soul, I'm blamed ef I wouldn't be dag-gone willin' to go right through it all and be killed again with them others to hear Marse Robert, dag-gone him, say over again as how he grieved bout'n we-all's losses and honored us for we-all's bravery! Darned ef I wouldn't." Isn't that reverential adoration, my darling, to be willing to be "killed again" for a word of praise?

It seems selfish and inhuman to speak of love—haunted as I am with the unnecessary sacrifice of the lives of so many of my brave boys. I can't think of anything but the desolate homes in Virginia and the unknown dead in Pennsylvania. At the beginning of the fight I was so sanguine, so sure of success! Early in the morning I had been assured by Alexander that General Lee had ordered that every brigade in his command was to charge Cemetery Hill; so I had no fear of not being supported. Alexander also assured me of the support of his artillery which would move ahead of my division in the advance. He told me that he had borrowed seven twelve-pound howitzers from Pendleton, Lee's Chief of Artillery, which he had put in reserve to accompany me.

In the morning I rode with him while he, by Longstreet's orders, selected the salient angle of the wood in which my line was formed, which line was just on the left of his seventy-five guns. At about a quarter to three o'clock, when his written order to make the charge was handed to me, and dear Old Peter after reading it in sorrow and fear reluctantly bowed his head in assent, I obeyed, leading my three brigades straight on the enemy's front. You never saw anything like it. They moved across that field of death as a battalion marches forward in line of battle upon drill, each commander in front of his command leading and cheering on his men. Two lines of the enemy's infantry were driven back; two lines of guns were taken—and no support came. Pendleton, without Alexander's knowledge, had sent four of the guns which he had loaned him to some other part of the field, and the other three guns could not be found. The two brigades which were to have followed me had, poor fellows, been seriously engaged in the fights of the two previous days. Both of their commanding officers had been killed, and while they had been replaced by gallant, competent officers,

*Two lines of their infantry
were driven back; two lines of
guns were taken—and no support came.—Page 106.*

these new leaders were unknown to the men.

Ah, if I had only had my other two brigades a different story would have been flashed to the world. It was too late to retreat, and to go on was death or capture. Poor old Dick Garnett did not dismount, as did the others of us, and he was killed instantly, falling from his horse. Kemper, desperately wounded, was brought from the field and subsequently, taken prisoner. Dear old Lewis Armistead, God bless him, was mortally wounded at the head of his command after planting the flag of Virginia within the enemy's lines. Seven of my colonels were killed, and one was mortally wounded. Nine of my lieutenant colonels were wounded, and three lieutenant colonels were killed. Only one field officer of my whole command, Colonel Cabell, was unhurt, and the loss of my company officers was in proportion.

I wonder, my dear, if in the light of the Great Eternity we shall any of us feel this was for the best and shall have learned to say, "Thy will be done."

No castles to-day, sweetheart. No, the

bricks of happiness and the mortar of love must lie untouched in this lowering gloom. Pray, dear, for the sorrowing ones.

YOUR SOLDIER.

Headquarters, July 12, 1863.

HEADQUARTERS, A. N. Va.,
July 9th, 1863.

General:

Your letter of the 8th has been received. It was with reluctance that I imposed upon your gallant division the duty of carrying prisoners to Staunton. I regretted to assign them to such a service, as well as to separate them from the Army, though temporarily, with which they have been so long and efficiently associated. Though small in numbers, their worth is not diminished, and I had supposed that the division itself would be loth to part from its comrades, at a time when the presence of every man is so essential.

No one grieves more than I do at the loss suffered by your noble division in the recent conflict, or honors it more for its bravery and gallantry. It will afford me hereafter satisfaction, when an opportunity occurs, to do all in my power to recruit its diminished ranks, and to recognize it in the most efficient manner.

Very respectfully, your obedient servant,

R. E. LEE, General.

Major Gen. G. E. Pickett, commanding,
Forwarded through Lieut. Gen. Longstreet.
C. MARSHALL, Major and A. D. C.

XXII

On the Way to Richmond—Guarding Prisoners

IT would be impossible, my darling, to describe to you even the half of the horrors and hardships of these last days, from the first night's long march to the present hour; not only for ourselves but for the prisoners whom, with shattered hopes and heartbreak we, the little remnant of my division, have been assigned to guard. "One prisoner is too many for us, who haven't a crust to go around among ourselves," as Old Jack said.

Oh, the pity of it, guarding these prisoners through their own country, depleted and suffering mentally and physically as we are, and being forced to march forward with a speed beyond their own and our endurance. It may be some consolation to both that we suffer alike from fatigue, hunger, exhaustion and wet, for the excessive rains which set in on the fourth have continued unabated.

THE HEART OF A SOLDIER

The long wagon-trains, the artillery, the assortment of vehicles of all kinds impressed from the farmers and loaded to their utmost capacity with our wounded and, anon, room made for the crowding in of yet another, falling from illness or exhaustion all along our way, have added their quota to the discomforts of the march. Our commissariat, too, has been as wretched here in this land of plenty as it was in the barren, war-ridden land we left behind. Our banquets, we, the guard of honor, and our guests, the prisoners, have shared like-and-like, and none was ever more enjoyed by either than the flour made into paste and baked on the stones in front of the fire and the good Pennsylvania beef roasted on the end of a stick. By the way, my Sally, when you are my little housekeeper you must remember that this stick-end roasting is a mighty toothsome recipe for cooking beef.

The prisoners have been far more cheerful than we have been, for they have not only had strong hope of being retaken by their own arms within a few days but their army has gained a great victory, and though dearly bought, it has, I fear, decided the fate of our new-born nation. The cannonading on the second morning, the shells from which we could clearly see bursting somewhere in the vicinity of the Monterey House and which we learned were from Kilpatrick's artillery, endeavoring to cut off our trains and prevent our retreat, gave the prisoners double assurance of release. Their hope of rescue being deferred at Monterey Springs, I instructed my Inspector-General to parole the officers and give them safeguard to return, binding them to render themselves prisoners of war at Richmond if they were not duly recognized by their government. Unfortunately, I was not permitted to release them at this point and they were required to march with the rest of the prisoners.

A Colonel of a Maine regiment, Colonel Tilden, a splendid, gallant fellow, so appreciative, too, of the very few small courtesies which it has been possible to show him, asked that I cancel their paroles, the main object of which had been to avoid the terrors of the march, which I, in honor, did of course.

Late in the evening after another trying day's march we passed Waynesboro and, with a rest of only an hour or so, marched all night. At nine o'clock the following morning we reached Hagerstown but hurried on through to Williamsport. All along the road from Hagerstown to Williamsport were gruesome evidences of Kilpatrick's dash into Hagerstown—here a dead cavalryman, there a broken caisson, a dead horse. I ought not to let your beautiful eyes see through mine all these horrors, but some day, my darling, some day we'll strew roses and violets and lilies over them all, even over the memories of them. We'll listen to the resurrection that hope and faith and love voice in all the songs of nature. It will not be long, darling, for to-day the official news of the surrender of Vicksburg reached us. The tidings brought cheers from the prisoners and increased the sullen gloom of their guard.

I am directed to turn the prisoners over to General Imboden's command, who is to escort them to Staunton. Their final destination will, I suppose, be the old nine-room brick warehouse on Carey Street in Richmond, "Libby & Sons—Ship Chandlers and Grocers"—a sign which I remember as a boy and associate with "Cat" and "Truant" and other boyish games. Always I shall like to remember it as a place to play, and not think of it as a living tomb. There will not, I fear, be many of my fellow-sufferers of the last few days who enter these awesome walls who will ever come forth alive.

The Potomac was so swollen by the rains which began on the fourth and still continue, that it was impossible to cross it at any of the neighboring fords. A rope ferry, the only means of crossing, made it slow and tedious, and every minute's delay, my darling, seems centuries when I am on my way to you—to you.

Jackerie has waited so long for my post-script that he has gone to sleep and I have now not time to write it, but you will know that the most important thing is in the P. S. and this is love,—the love of

Your adoring
SOLDIER.

On the March, July 12, 1863.

PART THREE

Wedding Bells that Rang in the Wilderness

*W*ITH the return of the army to Virginia, after the tragic defeat at Gettysburg, began the slow ebb of the tide that had carried the hopes of the Confederacy so high. It was in this crisis when he was back in his war-wasted state, fighting despondency and needing, as never before, the love and devotion of a wife that General Pickett determined to wait no longer but to marry his sweetheart at once. As he could not go to her she crossed the enemy's lines and joined him at Petersburg, where they were made one.

Soon after their marriage came the inevitable orders to march and the General and his bride were separated for weeks at a time. But his letters brought to her constant cheer and the promise, oft repeated, to come back to her in spite of the dangers besetting him. That he did so, was due certainly to some kind fortune that guarded him, since the deeds of daring which he performed at the head of his division became a tradition in the Army.

XXIII

In Which the General Issues An Order

OLD Peter is to go to Tennessee to reënforce Bragg. He has placed his plans
before the Secretary of War.

Now, my darling, I have just had a long
powwow with him (Old Peter) who, "old
war-horse" as he is, has been in love himself,
is still in love, will always be in love, and
knows of our love—of our plighted troth—
and knowing it, tells me it is his purpose to
take me with him on this proposed expedition.

Now, my Sally, your Soldier is a soldier,
and never, even to himself, questions an order.
"His not to reason why." Darling, do you
know what this means? Why, my little one,
it means that you haven't one moment's res-
pite. It means that you are to be Mrs. General George Pickett, my precious wife, right
away. It means that you are to fulfill your

117

promise to "come to me at a moment's notice."
Yours, too, *now,* "not to reason why," but to
obey and come at once. We cannot brook
any delay, my darling; so pack up your knap-
sack—never mind the rations and the ammunition, but come. My Aunt Olivia, with
Uncle Andrew, one of my staff and one of my
couriers will meet you and your dear parents
on this side of the Black Water and will escort
you to Petersburg, where I shall be waiting
at the train to meet you. I shall see you all
to the hotel, where you will wait while your
father, Bright and I get the license and make
other necessary arrangements for our imme-
diate marriage, which I have planned to take
place *sine die* at St. Paul's Church. Our
old friend, Doctor Platt, will pronounce
the words that make us one in the sight of the
world. From the church, we will go to the
depot, where a special train, having been arranged for us by our friend, Mr. Reuben
Raglan, God bless him, will take us over to
Richmond, where my little sister is waiting
longingly to love and welcome my wife—her
new sister.

My darling will realize how impossible it

THE HEART OF A SOLDIER

is for her Soldier to consult with her and will forgive his bungling and awkwardness. Never mind, after this *she* shall do *all* the planning. Oh, what a heaven on earth is before us—if only this cruel war were over! A Dios. Forgive this business letter. Courier awaits. You will come; I have no fear.

Forever your

SOLDIER.

Headquarters, Sept. 13, 1863.

XXIV

Written After Their Marriage, on an Expedition Into North Carolina

IT seems an age, my darling, since we rode away, leaving you and Mrs. Ransom[1] standing in that wonderful grove of maiden trees. I veil the annoying, disappointing scenes since then and see again the beautiful picture of my own bride, clothed in white, in the greenery with the "grandfather squirrels" playing all around her, climbing over her and eating from her dainty, graceful hands. "Mine—mine—all my own!" I said, invoking our Father's care of you. Oh, my love, all my happiness is in your hands, and as you love me, guard your precious self from all harm. I have you on my heart all the day.

Ransom sent on our letters from Kingston, via the Ugr.[2] I hope they reached you safely.

[1] Wife of General Ransom.
[2] Underground railway.

Old Floyd[3] sent a most mysterious looking package to you and Mrs. Ransom, which he said you must both thank St. Paul for. In Floyd's opinion, St. Paul has as much to answer for as the great Apostle for whom he is named. Certainly in appearance he is as insignificant looking as a horse as St. Paul has been described as a man, and while he has not had one, much less five, shipwrecks, he has had all manner of hairbreadth escapes, hardships, indignities and a million times more stripes, all of which he has borne with Christian resignation and endurance.

Well, dearest, my name is George and my patience and temper accord with the name. Our well-formed plans for the capture of Newbern miscarried. Hoke's, Clingman's and Corse's Brigades and Reid's Artillery under my command were to make a feint—to threaten on the south side of the Neuse River. Dearing's Cavalry and three regiments of infantry under Dearing were to make a demonstration on the north side of the Neuse. Ransom, Barton, and Terry under Barton were to make the *real* attack, while we created a diver-

3 Headquarters Sutler.

sion and drew off the enemy. Simultaneously with our movements Colonel R. Taylor Wood was to take a naval force in small boats, make a night excursion down the Neuse and attack the gunboats. The soldiers were all jubilant, buoyant and hopeful. Everything was propitious; victory seemed sure. General Dearing's feint was successful. Hoke and Corse and Clingman crossed over, taking all the defenses and outworks in front. Wood's attack was a complete surprise, capturing a gunboat right under the guns of the fort; but, alas, the *real* attack by Barton was not made. We waited in deathlike suspense. Hour after hour of restless anxiety and impatience went by and yet no sound of a gun—and no message came to tell me why. The torture and suspense were unbearable. Newbern was ours—ours if— Well—hope died out and the dejection and despair of the men with their hopes dashed cannot be told.

As ever,

YOUR SOLDIER.

XXV

From the Lines Near Petersburg, Va.

YOUR Soldier breathes easier this morning, my darling. A great load is lifted. Haygood's brave South Carolina Brigade came in yesterday, thank God, and I stationed them at Port Walthall Junction. This will keep the connection between Petersburg and Richmond open. Wise's Brigade got in today and was sent out toward City Point.

For nights I have not closed my eyes. How could I, with a whole city full of helpless, defenseless women and children at the mercy of an oncoming army? Butler's whole force, in transports protected by his gunboats, landed at City Point and Bermuda Hundred, and no army here to meet them! Not enough soldiers, boys and old men all put together, even for picket duty!

Come to think of it, my prettice, you must have been up all night to have made up and

sent out such a basket of goodies, and baked
and buttered such a lot of biscuits, and made
so many jugs of coffee as came this morning.
My, I tell you it all tasted good, and the
coffee—well, no Mocha or Java ever tasted
half so good as this rye-sweet-potato blend!
And think of your thoughtfulness in wrapping
blankets around the jugs to keep the coffee
hot. Bless your thoughtful heart! You are,
without doubt, the dearest, most indefatigable
little piece of perfection that ever rode a
horse or buttered a biscuit or plucked a flower
or ever did anything else, as to that. Then
those hyacinths and geranium leaves! Who
else in all this nerve-racking, starving, perilous
time would have thought of gathering flowers?
My nigger, Bob, the loyal but unappreciative
scamp, apologetically took out the baskets,
which were apparently filled with the yet dew-
kissed fragrant flowers, and said:

"Miss Sallie, Marse George, de Mistis,
done en sont you all dese yer endoubled
hyacinfs. En I axed her huccome she sont
'em; but she didn't say. So ef you all don't
lak 'em you-all mus' 'scuse her fer it en put
all de blame 'pon me. En anyhow, Marse

George, ef you cyan't eat dese hyacinfses ner w'ar 'em ner shoot de Yankees wid' em, dey suttinly does smell good and dey sho' is pretty."

Mrs. Stratton and Mrs. Johnson sent out large hampers, too, to us. They came just after we had finished with your baskets, and we passed them on to others.

And now, my darling, what on earth did you mean by saying, "Never mind," as you said good-by and rode away yesterday. It troubled me all night. I wanted to follow after you and ask you what you meant, but couldn't. I would have jumped on Lucy and ridden in to Petersburg and found out if it had been *possible* for me to leave. I was so troubled about it that I was almost tempted to come in anyhow. For the life of me, little one, I couldn't think of any reason why you should say, "Never mind," to *me*. Were you aggrieved because your blundering old Soldier told you there was no necessity for your coming out to bring the dispatches, any longer; that, thank heaven, the recruits and reënforcements were coming in now, and that we could manage all right? I did not mean to hurt you, dear.

THE HEART OF A SOLDIER

I hoped you'd send a line by Bob telling me what you meant and why you had said it, but when I asked him if you had written, he said:

"Yes, Suh, Marse George, 'course de mistis is done en writ a letter er a answer er sumpin'; but ef she did done it, den I mus' er forgot ter fotch it, bein' ez I wuz in sich a hurry ter git yere in time dis mornin' wid de baskets, en startin' befo' daybre'k. En den dis ebenin' a gettin' de basket en papers en milk en things ready in sich a hurry agin, I mus' er forgot de letter agin."

Now, please, my darling, send Bob back *right away* with a nice letter and tell your Soldier that you did not mean anything by saying, "Never mind," to him, for he loves you with all his heart and would not wound or disappoint or offend you for anything in the world.

YOUR SOLDIER.

On the Lines, May 7, 1864.

XXVI

In the Wilderness Before Cold Harbor

BAIRD has just come in from the lines, my darling wife, and reports that all is well. I came in about eleven and was lying in my tent all alone, thinking of you, and while I builded wonderful castles I was serenading you with the songs I love.

I think I had finished all the songs I had ever sung to you, and when Baird came in my thoughts had wandered to the Salmon-Illahie and I was singing Anne Boleyn's song, "Oh Death, Rock Me Asleep," which was taught me by my friend, Captain G. P. Hornby, of Her Majesty's ship *Tribune,* away out in San Juan Island on the Pacific Coast in 1859. I do not know why I was singing this song, except that it is beautiful and one of the finest and sweetest of melodies. Both the air and words were written by poor, unfortunate Anne Boleyn. I know but one verse—if

Hornby ever knew other verses he had forgotten them—but the one I know is appealing.   I will write it for you, if I may:

"Oh, Death, rock me asleep!   Bring me to quiet and rest;
Let pass my weary, guiltless life out of my careful breast;
Toll on the passing bell, ring out my doleful knell;
Let thy sound my death tell.   Death doth draw me,
Death doth draw me.   There is no remedy."

Baird stopped outside and listened and then
came in, asking permission to order Bob to
light the dips, and saying, "Please, Sir, Marse
George, when you sing that song I haven't got
a friend in the world.   I'm lonesome and feel
creeps and see spooks and, what's worse, I
don't know whether I am Anne Boleyn herself, or am myself responsible for all poor
Anne's sorrows and death."

So I stopped singing and am writing to tell
you a great secret, which is—I love you.
Some day when we are happy—so happy that
nothing could make us any happier—I'll sing
this song to you.

Last night there was a night attack.   Several of the men were wounded slightly; but
the face of one—perhaps seriously wounded—

haunts me. He is a boy with golden brown curls—somebody's darling. To-night, we made a capture of the Federal pickets, sweeping their rifle-pits for more than a hundred yards and taking a hundred and thirty-six prisoners. You know our lines are so close together in many places that we, the Yankees and my men, can with voices raised carry on a conversation.

War and its horrors, and yet I sing and whistle. Oh, my sweetheart, if only this wicked war were over so that we could in peace and quiet tranquilly finish the book of Love which we have but just begun.

Adios now. I see old Jackerie in the flap with his pack and bag, his wonted grace and patience, his *dolce-far-niente* eyes and soft, southern Italian voice, saying, "No hulla-nonenty." But I must hurry, for he starts at daybreak and it is now past midnight.

Lovingly now and forever,
YOUR SOLDIER.

In Camp, June, 1864.

XXVII

Recalling a Visit from "Old Jack"

HERE we are still, my darling. My
division is stationed with the rest of the
First Corps between new and old Cold Harbor. Old Peter, having been wounded in the
Wilderness, Anderson has been put in command of the First Corps. Grant has been ap-
pointed Lieutenant General and has arrived
at nearly the same point in his march down
the river that McClellan reached in his up-
ward progress in '62. Over a crimson road
both armies have returned to Cold Harbor.
The Wilderness, alas, is one vast graveyard
where sleep thousands of Grant's soldiers; but
Grant, like our Stonewall, is "fighting not to
save lives, but country."

For the second time now Cold Harbor has
become a battle-ground. Two years ago it
furnished the field for the battle of Gaines's
Mill (which the Yankees called Cold Harbor) where your Soldier was wounded. Does

it seem to you as long ago as two years, my
darling? To me, it seems but yesterday that
I lay in Richmond at my little sister's and you
came to see me, blessing and cheering me. I
can feel now the soft touch of your little white
hands, as you gently stroked and soothed my
wounded shoulder and swollen arm and hand.
Do you remember one afternoon while you
were reading from Moore's melodies (not that
I heard or took in the meaning of a single word
of them, for I only heard the music of your
wonderful voice and saw the long, dark lashes
caressing the words which those cupid-shaped
cherry lips were uttering) that our dear old
Stonewall was announced? Of course I knew
his calling was out of the usual, and I was
honored and gratified by his coming; but any
guest was unwelcome if I had to share with
him my darling. I remember that you
marked the place you were reading with your
dainty, scented handkerchief, which I stole
and still have. You and my sister were about
to withdraw; but both the General and I
urged you to remain. I shall always hold
sacred "Old Jack's" visit and remember its
every detail.

Do you recall how indignant our maid-servant was at what she supposed a reflection upon the mint-juleps she was serving? You remember the uncompromising, stern old Puritan declined, saying, "Take that liquor away. I never touch strong drink. I like it too well to fool with it, and no man's strength is strong enough to touch that stuff with impunity." You remember how, though she politely curtsied, poor Julie, humbly but vigorously defending her juleps, replied, " 'Scuse me, Marse Gen'ul Jackson, but dese yer drams ain't got no impunities in 'em, Suh. Nor, Suh. Braxton done en mek 'em out'n we-all's ve'y bes' old London Dock brandy out'n one of we-all's cobweb bottles."

Old Jackerie brought me your letter on the first, just after the Yankees' attack on Hoke and Kershaw, breaking their outer lines. That night Grant transferred his right to a point beyond Cold Harbor. On the afternoon of the second Marse Robert ordered an assault on Grant's right; but old Jubal found it invincible and went to work erecting defenses. I believe it was old Jube who gave Marse Robert the title of "Old-Spades-Lee," or "Old

Ace of Spades," because of his incessant activity in throwing up defenses, trenches, breastworks, etc. This morning Grant made an assault along the entire six miles of our line, and our guns opened a counter attack, followed by advance skirmishes of my division. The whole Confederate line poured a stream of fire, and thousands of Grant's soldiers have gone to reënforce the army of the dead.

Oh, this is all a weary, long mistake. May the merciful and true God wield power to end it ere another day passes!

YOUR SOLDIER.

Cold Harbor, June 3, 1864.

XXVIII

*After General Lee Had Congratulated His
Division for Gallantry*

OUTSIDE, my darling, the band has been
playing the songs that we love, and inside I have been softly singing them all to
you, to your spirit far away. Now they have
wound up with "Alice, Where Art Thou?"
which might have set me wondering if it had
not been the hour we each seek to be alone that
we may bring our souls in touch. So I knew
that thou wert with me.

This morning Tom Friend brought me a
weesome package of tea, which he wishes sent
to you. "One of the men," he said, "swapped
his tobacco for it." If the whole universe
were mine, I'd lay it at your feet, for love has
builded in my heart three altars for thy worship—one to Faith, one to Hope, one to Service—and you, my Goddess whom I worship,
must feed my faith, illumine my hope and
command my service.

This morning, for reasons which you will presently note, I was thinking of our ever memorable ride from Petersburg. Its anxieties and pleasures, your indomitable pluck and merry laughter on that day pass before me, making me shudder with fear or thrill with happiness. It was on your birthday, you remember, and Beauregard had been forced to leave his intrenchments at early daylight, and Butler had walked into them and had succeeded in reaching the Richmond and Petersburg Railroad and was destroying the track when the advance guard of my division ran him off. I had left you in the rear and had gone on about a quarter of a mile in advance of my division and was riding quietly along with the members of my staff and General R. H. Anderson, who was then commanding the corps. We were some ten miles or so from Petersburg when we were ambushed and fired into by a portion of Butler's troops. Hunton's Brigade was followed up by my other brigades, and we drove the enemy back toward Bermuda Hundred, where they were stopped by my men who retook the whole line.

This gallant and unexpected action so

pleased Marse Robert that he yesterday had published the inclosed notice, which I send you that you may be reminded of my glorious, fearless men who yet survived that awful third of July where so many of their comrades were left to sleep. The line of breastworks which they took and to which Marse Robert refers in the notice inclosed is most important, as the main line of defense between Richmond and Petersburg and opposing any advance of the enemy upon the peninsula of Bermuda Hundred.

Now my darling sees why I am thinking of that 16th of May. It was because she, though Marse Robert doesn't know it, comes in for a share of his praise. I am thinking of you every minute and wish that I could ride in, if only for an hour between sundown and midnight, to see you; but, to use Mr. Lincoln's expressive words, Grant is so "infernally interruptious" that I am afraid to take the risk.

Now, my strayed angel of the skies, don't be disappointed. I love you. Good night. May all blessings bless you, all sunshine shine for you, all angels guard you, all that is good take care of you and all heaven help me to be worthy of you.

Forever and ever

YOUR SOLDIER.

Headquarters, June 18, 1864.

Clay's House, 5:30 P. M., June 17, 1864.

LIEUTENANT-GENERAL R. H. ANDERSON,

Commanding Longstreet's Corps.

GENERAL:

I take great pleasure in presenting to you my congratulations upon the conduct of the men of your corps. I believe they will carry anything they are put against. We tried very hard to stop Pickett's men from capturing the breastworks of the enemy, but could not do it. I hope his loss has been small.

I am, with respect, your obedient servant,

R. E. LEE, General.

XXIX

When Butler Burned the General's Old Home

WAS my letter of yesterday strenuous?
Well, it was a strenuous day, full of
rumors and contradictions. And yet in spite
of it I managed to sandwich in between the
shelling and the movement of the fleet and
the distinguished visitors the ever new and
true story of my love. But I had only time
to make the bare announcement at the close of
that letter that Butler had burned our home
the day before. If it had been burned in line
of battle, it would have been all right; but it
was not. It was burned by Butler at a great
expense to the Government and in revenge
for having been outgeneraled by a little handful of my men at Petersburg and for Grant's
telegram to Mr. Lincoln, saying, "Pickett has
bottled up Butler at Petersburg."

Mr. Sims, who has been our overseer ever
since I can remember, came up from Turkey

Island this morning to tell me all about it. The poor old fellow loved the old place and is heartbroken over its destruction. He says they first looted the house and then shelled and burned it, together with the barn and stables. He is very bitter and vindictive and vows all manner of eternal vengeance. The poor old chap is sensitive because I did not rave and rage with him, and resents what he considers my indifference. He gave me the benefit of all the swear words in his vocabulary when I tried to make him understand that there are weightier things and subjects of greater moment than the mere loss of personal property.

" 'Personal property!' " he quoted indignantly. "Why, Turkey Island was your ma's and pa's and their ma's and pa's before 'em. Think of them big oaks, them maiden trees, the river and everything! Think of all the big men that's set 'round that old mahogany table and jingled their glasses at that big old sideboard! 'Personal property!' Why, when you was just a turning six your pa and me showed you the very halting place whar in January, 1781, that traitor, Benedict Arnold, stopped on his march to Richmond after he had come up with the fleet at Jamestown and then went on to Westover. 'Personal property!' Why, I remember the very day we sot you up in the crotch of that great old oak tree under which Governor Jefferson and Mr. Edmund Randolph 'lighted from their fillies and tied them to one of the limbs till they could walk a piece and see for themselves that old monument put up in 1711, eleven years before that time, to show how much devilment a river could do if it had the elements to help it. 'Personal property!' Why, Sir, there wan't a picture or a piece of furniture or a statuary in that old home that wan't only seasoned with age, but had a store of valuableness to it besides, and you passive and peaceable, taking the news all quiet as if it had been nothing but a fence rail burnt up, and telling me to my face, and me a-bustin' out with damnation from every pore, that you had heard of the fire, that Mr. Enroughty had reported the burning of Turkey Island yesterday! 'Reported!' 'Personal property!' I wonder if a man's soul is personal property. Well, if it is and Mr. Satan should ever report to me that he wanted any help to keep up his fire to burn

Mr. Butler's, or any of his kind of personal property, he would know where to get it!"

Poor Mr. Sims! I've sent him with one of my couriers to find some of his friends in the trenches, where I hope he will work off some of his wrath over Butler and his kind and my unfortunate phrase "personal property." Of course you know, my darling, that I am not unmindful of the sacredness of the old home and that I grieve that it has been destroyed, but we will build us another home, won't we? The river is there, and some of the old trees are left. And if God should bless us with a son I shall, when he is as old as I was then, take him under this same old historic tree that Mr. Sims speaks of and tell him in the very language of my father some of the old stories he used to tell me, and introduce him to the great men of those days as my father made me acquainted with them. I can hear him now say:

"My son, there was Madison, a very, very small man with introverted eyes and ample forehead. He dressed always in a surtout of brown, which was generally dusty and oftener than otherwise faded and shabby. Judge Marshall was very tall and commanding and revolutionary and patriarchal in appearance. He had fine expressive eyes and dressed always in a well-fitting surtout of blue. Mr. John Randolph was puny and frail and most uncommon looking. He was swarthy and wrinkled, with eyes as brilliant as stars of the first magnitude. Watkins Leigh was unusually distinguished in appearance. Tazewell was tall and fine looking; but Mr. Monroe was very wrinkled and weather-beaten and so exceedingly awkward that he stumbled over his own feet and walked on everyone else's. Governor Giles used a crutch always and talked like molasses in July."

My father never used made-up words or a children's vocabulary in describing to me men and events. He would say, "Words are things, my son. I want you to know them and not be like the British officer who, when he and some of his command were taken prisoners and were told by their captors that they were to be paroled, demanded in great terror and consternation, "Pray, what kind of death is that?'"

Oh, my Sally, I dream of the happy days when you will be the fair mistress of Turkey

Island, under those old trees, with the James River always before us and love always with us. As the sun in the firmament, so is love in the world—love, the life of the spirit, the root of every virtuous action. It enhanceth prosperity, easeth adversity and maketh of the slightest twist a Gordian knot. It gives vigor to the atmosphere, fragrance to the flower, color to the rainbow, zest to life, music to laughter, and oh, such laughter as yours, my own, my beautiful. I love you with all my heart and soul and mind and being. A Dios. Keep this love close.

YOUR SOLDIER.

Headquarters, June —, 1864.

PART FOUR

In the Shadow of the End

*T*HE long struggle between the states was now drawing to a close. The South, depleted in men and resources, awaited in grim despair the failure of its hopes. Gloom and disappointment settled down upon all, men and officers alike, but to General Pickett there came a gleam of happiness in the birth of his son. The event was one that was hailed with rejoicing on both sides of the battle lines— for the contending armies were but paces apart. Grant and his staff sent a birthday greeting to the "Little General," as the boy was dubbed immediately, and though the armies met again in conflict the incident served to lessen the feeling that had existed between them. A brief nine months later, Pickett wrote: "Peace is born."

XXX

Upon Hearing of the Birth of the "Little General"

GOD bless you, little Mother of our boy—bless and keep you. Heaven in all its glory shine upon you; Eden's flowers bloom eternal for you. Almost with every breath since the message came, relieving my anxiety and telling me that my darling lived and that a little baby had been born to us, I have been a baby myself. Though I have known all these months that from across Love's enchanted land this little child was on its way to our twin souls, now that God's promise is fulfilled and it has come, I can't believe it. As I think of it I feel the stir of Paradise in my senses, and my spirit goes up in thankfulness to God for this, His highest and best—the one perfect flower in the garden of life—Love.

Blinding tears rolled down my cheeks, my

sweetheart, as I read the glad tidings. And a feeling so new, so strange, came over me that I asked of the angels what it could be and whence came the strains of celestial music which filled my soul, and what were the great, grand, stirring hosannas and the soft, tender, sweet adagios that circled round and round, warmed my every vein, beat in my every pulse. And—oh, little Mother of my boy—the echoing answer came—"A little baby has been born to you, and he and the new-born Mother live."

I wanted to fly to you both, kneel by your bedside, take your hand and his little hand in mine and lift our hearts in thankfulness to the Heavenly Throne. But when I applied to the great Tyee for a pass to Richmond, saying, "My son was born this morning," he replied, "Your country was born almost a hundred years ago." It was the first word of reproach Marse Robert ever spoke to me; but he was right and I was reckless to ask.

Things may be quieter to-morrow, sweetheart, perhaps even to-night, and I may be able to come in for an hour. I must not write another word, though I want to write on and

on and send messages and kisses to the little
baby and to caution its Mother to be careful
and to tell her she is ten thousand times more
precious than ever, but I must not.

Lovingly and forever and ever

YOUR SOLDIER.

July 17, 1864—Our boy's birthday.
Blessed Day.

XXXI

A Second Letter on His Son's Birthday.

GOD has heard our prayers, my beloved
wife. Oh, the ecstatic pleasure I felt
when Charles brought the Doctor's letter.
Precious one, you must obey every injunction
of our dear Aunt. Do not think of writing or
exerting yourself in any way. She knows all
about what should be done. I am coming to
you this evening, should General Lee say so,
and he will, for I have sent Bright post haste
to him, telling him of the glory of the Star in
the East.

Oh, my pretty wife! I long to see you and
your little son—*Our* son! Little new-born
mother, I have humbly thanked God for His
great and bounteous goodness; every breath I
breathe is one of gratitude to Him for sparing you to me and giving us a son—thou Life
of my soul. Ever and forever

YOUR DEVOTED SOLDIER.

Sunday, 17th July.
Blessed Day!

XXXII

On the Occasion of His First Visit to His Boy

MY men had all heard of the arrival of the "Little General," as they call him, and when I was riding out of camp last night to surrender to him, I noticed the bonfires which were being kindled all along my lines and knew that my loyal, loving men were lighting them in honor of my baby. But I did not know till this morning that dear old Ingalls, at Grant's suggestion, had kindled a light on the other side of the lines, too, and I was overcome with emotion when I learned of it. To-day their note of congratulation, marked unofficial, which I inclose, came to me through the lines. You must keep it for the baby, with the pass and note of Marse Robert which I put into its little clenched hand.

"Baby!" Can it be true, my darling? Heaven knows no deeper devotion, no deeper gratitude, than that which filled my heart when I realized that the golden dream of life had come to pass—was true; when I looked upon the sweet, shy face of my girl bride and saw it transformed into the sacred tenderness of motherhood, saw the grace and charm, the soul-born protecting look in the mother eyes, the lilied sweetness of her face, the smile of unlanguaged mystery, with a gentleness and patience as sweet and meek as Mother Mary wore. I knew it was the Alpha and Omega of Heaven.

I see still the moss rose bud left by the *Blumen-Engel* as a *bescheidenen Schmuck* of his love nestling in your snow-white arms and the long, dark lashes kissing your cheeks as you look down upon it. I still feel the mystic power of the grasp of its tiny rose leaf fingers clutched around my own.

But I must not write another word—not one.   Lovingly,
                                          YOUR SOLDIER.
In Camp, July 19, 1864.

To GEORGE PICKETT:
We are sending congratulations to you, to the young mother and the young recruit.
                              GRANT, INGALLS, SUCKLEY.
    July 18, 1864.

XXXIII

Upon Returning from a Ride With Marse Robert

I HAVE but a few moments since, my pretty one, returned from a ride with the Tyee up one hill and down the other. The enemy occupied Dutch Gap last evening. This is higher up the river than I am and I had expected the Navy to take care of our rear but they have allowed them to come in, and now I have to stretch out my India rubber division.

Well, my pet, I *have* to do it. The General did not seem in a remarkably good humor— with the news from Mobile and Bradley, Johnson in the valley, and this impudence of the Yankees in crawling up behind us.

I am so glad, my own, that you are better— thank the good God for it. Blair says you must not keep the baby in your arms so much, that you are acting mother and nurse both.

153

THE HEART OF A SOLDIER

Please listen to the doctor this time, and to your husband's pleading. Blair says that his indisposition is nothing but the colic, and that you must not make yourself uneasy about the little fellow. You *must* make Lucinda nurse him more.

I send you a chicken, a cup of salt, likewise an apple—one single one. Your friend, Miss Gamble, radiant with a white frock and smiles, sent it to me (*didn't give it*) with her compliments last night.

Bye-bye, Sweet One.

Ever your own
SOLDIER.

Headquarters, August —, 1864.

XXXIV

Concerning the Gossip of His Servant, George

I LEFT you yesterday, my darling, "with many a pause and longing glance behind"; but out in the midst of this terrible conflict to which I have come, your love is with me, shielding and blessing me.

I reached camp just before daybreak. George hustled around and made me a pot of "sho'nough coffee wid no debultrement in it." And while I drank my coffee he kept off the flies—which, early as it was, had begun to be very sociable—entertaining me the while with news of the camp and his own views on current events.

"You know, Marse George," he began, "po' Robert, Marse Jefferson Davis' mos' betrusted servant, is done en bruck out thick all ober wid de smallpox, en dar ain' no tellin' how many er de President's friends en 'quaintances po' Robert is done en kernockulated wid it, kaze po' Robert wuz moughty sociable and familious wid all de President's friends. I suttinly hopes dat you en Gen'l Lee en Gen'l Heth is gwine ter 'scape. I wuz so upsot, Marse George, by dis news 'bout po' Robert dat I couldn't sleep, en I got out behime de tent en listened ter de officers a talkin' wid dar moufs en gesticulatin' 'bout de way t'ings wuz gwine.

"Some er 'em said how ef Marse Albert Sydney Johnston hadn't been kilt at Shiloh, en ef Marse Joe Johnston hadn't been wounded at Seben Pines, en ef you had been s'ported at Gettysburg, dat t'ings wouldn't be lak dey wuz now. Den one er de officers say, 'Yes—yes, en ef all er dem folks down dar in New 'Leans dat commit suicide wid darse'fs, 'count er ole Butler's pusecution en hangin's en yuther devilments, had er kilt him fust fo' dey kilt deyse'fs dey'd er had sumpin ter die fer, en de ole rascal wouldn't be down here now adiggin' dis Dutch-Gap-Canal en givin ev'body ague en fever turnin' up de earf!' Den one er de preacher officers say, 'Well, my frien's, de trouble is, we all don' pray enough!' Marse Charley spuck up en say, 'Didn't Gen'l

Jackson pray enough fer us all, Colonel?'
Nur one say, 'Yes, Charley, but he didn't dust
his knees off when he wuz through. He forgot dat bein' clean wuz nex' ter being Godli-
some.' Den a nur one say, 'Well, but dar's
ole Gen'l Pemberton en Gen'l Kershaw.
Dey wuz particular wid dar clothes en dey
prayed all right.' Den Gen'l Corse he spuck
up en say, 'Yes, but dey bofe think *too much*
'bout dar 'pearance. Dey'd begin to dus' en
dus' dar knees fo' dey said, "Amen." En dat
showed dar hearts wan't in dar prayers.'

"En gwine back, Marse George, ter dat
Dutch-Gap-Canal, you know Colonel Mayo's
nigger, Big Joe, en sebenteen mo' er de camp
niggers is done en gone 'cross de river ter
jine de Yankee Army en he'p de res' er dem
Yankee-nigger soldiers ter dig dat canal ditch
dey's diggin' er 'count er all dat extra
money en extra drams en coffee en yuther
extras Gen'l Butler promise ter give 'em.
Now, Marse George, you know dat dat's
projickin' wid de Lord's handy works, en
sumpin mousterious en terrible is gwine ter
happen ter dem niggers. Diggin' dat canal
sho'ly is gwine ag'inst de judgment er de

157

Lord, fer ef de Lord had er wanted de Jeemes River ter a jined on ter itse'f He'd a jined it. He wouldn't a put a little slice er land in betwixt. En sho's you're bawn projickin' wid de Lord's work en unj'inin' whut He's j'ined tergedder ain' a gwine ter bring dem niggers no proskerity."

Having finished my breakfast George went out to get breakfast for the mess, and before they had assembled I had cleared off my desk and written several letters. All made affectionate inquiries for you and our little son, though some of them did not know that I had ridden in last night until I told them.

I must go now, my darling, and ride around the lines and make my report, but will add a few more words later on. So adios till then.

. . . .

Well, my darling, we have had a most exciting day. Marse Robert came out. He was restive and very, very silent. We had just paid our respects to Butler's diggers when he arrived. The device we used in so doing was a new one or rather a very old one newly revived. It was a mortar battery hidden in the bushes. It is invisible to the enemy and easily shifted from one hiding place to the other. It used to be the only way in which shells could be thrown. It throws these shells high in the air, and they fall by their own weight without the least warning of their coming. There is no screaming or squealing sound like that made by our modern shells. They fall almost as silently as a snowflake falls, and it seems to me almost barbarous to drop these silent, ghostly missiles down upon those light-hearted, happy-go-lucky negroes, for I learn that it is they that are doing the digging. Butler, with promise of extra pay for extra work and extra danger, has induced four hundred of the colored soldiers to volunteer to sheathe their swords and take up the shovel and go to digging.

The bank to be cut through is only about five feet at the highest point. The canal is to be where the James makes a great bend just above Dutch Gap, inclosing a point of land perhaps half a mile wide and about three miles in length and which at the neck is only five hundred yards across from river to river. Their canal would thus save them six miles and would allow their gunboats to go up the James without running the gauntlet of our Howlett guns, our sunken torpedoes et cetera. And as our left is all at the turn of the bend, they would not have to traverse the open river in search of an exposed water channel. It is strange that some of our brilliant engineers haven't made this near cut years ago. As for me, I should encourage Butler and his River Improvement Company, and cease throwing these stealthy shells whose silent fall heralds a sudden roar of explosion that strikes terror to my soul. The canal will be an advantage to us, and Butler, in digging it for us, may in part atone for the many homes he has destroyed, mine among them.

Well, my darling, if you were not the best of all good women, as well as the most beautiful of all beautiful women and the most patient of all patient ones, you would weary of so tiresome a soldier, who takes away the fragrance of flowers and the glory of love and sends back the echo of war and its sorrows and the babble of a loyal old cook who wouldn't be sold and wouldn't run away and whom I was obliged to permit to be credited

THE HEART OF A SOLDIER

to me in order to save him—the only negro I
own—but, come to think of it, he owns me.

Forever and ever

YOUR SOLDIER.

In Camp, August —, 1864.

XXXV

After an Evening Spent at the "White House" of the Confederacy

YOU will be glad, my darling wife, that the "powwow" with "the Powers that be" was most satisfactory.

After the evening consultation I called on the ladies at the "White House" and at the most earnest entreaty and solicitation of Mrs. Davis and her sister, Miss Howell, dined with them. Poor Mr. Davis looks tired and anxious, but he spoke so hopefully of our success that, knowing, as he must know, our status, the condition of our army, etc., I should have thought that he was aware of something hopeful of which we are ignorant if he had not said later, when foreign intervention was being discussed, that he believed that England and, in fact, all the foreign powers were like the woman who saw her husband fighting a bear—she didn't care a continental which was whipped, but she'd be the best pleased if both were. "And my only hope of recognition," he said, "is that, being separated, we shall not be so formidable a power."

The dinner, my dearest, was beautiful, and so abundant were its luxuries that I marveled greatly, knowing, as I do, how difficult it is with most of us to get even a little tea or coffee or salt. As usual, Mrs. Davis was vivacious and entertaining. She amusingly described her rescue of a little orphan negro from a "great black brute" who had constituted himself the boy's guardian. She told how she had him washed and combed and dressed in a suit of little Joe's clothes, and how, while he was proud of the clothes, he was a thousand times prouder of, and more grateful for, the cuts and bruises which his self-appointed guardian had given him and which, upon all occasions, he triumphantly exhibited as medals of honor. She said that the little rascal was greatly troubled when the cuts were finally healed and tried to reopen them with a dog knife which was taken away. He was then reproved and forbidden to make over his wounds.

"Oh, Lordy," he howled, "ef you-all teks my sores 'way fum me I won't hab nuttin' 'tall ter show ter all de comp'ny, en I won't hab a single thing ter mek 'em all sorry 'bout, en nuttin' ter mek 'em gib me no mo' things. Oh, Lordy, I'd ruther you'd all whop me dan notter let me hab my sores no mo.' "

With her keen sense of humor Mrs. Davis told us how, when learning that one after another of her maids was being bribed by the Yankees with money and promises to betray the family and come over to the other side, she would pretend ignorance of the intention, give them food for imagination, reciting for their repetition the most impossible, outlandish stories, some of which she told us and which I will tell my darling when I come. Bless her! Mrs. Davis said that Betty, the last one of her maids to go, was such an excellent maid and so hard to replace that as soon as she began to show her prosperity, appearing with silks and jewels and then with gold and notes, she had tried, without letting Betty suspect her intention, to offer her inducements to remain, but had failed. Betty, she said, was superior to her class, however, and showed her con-

sideration by offering Miss Howell part of
the as yet unearned bribe, and assuring her
that "Ef eber I did git a chance ter tell dem
dar Yankees 'bout dey-all I suttinly aren't
gwine tell 'em none er de awful scand'lus
things I en Mrs. Davis was all de time a doin'
en dat dey all does. *No,* I am gwine ter mek
de best er hit en leave outn de worse."

Mrs. Davis said she was so depressed after
Betty's departure and in such dire need of
mental soothing syrup that she went into re-
tirement with "Adam Bede," "A Country
Gentleman in Town" and "Elective Affini-
ties." Did you ever, my darling!

Mr. Judah P. Benjamin and Dr. Minnegerode were the only other guests. Mr. Benjamin's usually wonderful, judicial mind and
depressing dignity were not in evidence. He
did rather reproachfully express his astonish-
ment that Mr. Davis should be bowed down
with grief at the adverse criticisms of those he
was trying to serve, and that he should care a
bauble for their accusations of nepotism and
the more absurd charge of leaving his cotton
to be bought by the Yankees. He ended by
saying that he continually had to remind Mr.

Davis of that exceedingly good man, Mr. Christ. You know Benjamin was born at St. Croix in the West Indies, of Jewish parents.

What a gossip your husband is, my Sally, but I promised to write my beautiful tyrant every day, everything I said or did or that anyone else said or did, and I have, haven't I?

Forever and ever and ever

YOUR SOLDIER.

Richmond, Jan. 25, 1865.

XXXVI

In the Dark Days Before the End

THIS morning at breakfast, my darling
Sally, when you suggested having an
oyster roast for my officers after our conference to-night, I said that I feared we should
not have enough oysters. Our old hunter,
Gossett, has just brought in a fine large wild
turkey, and with that and the three bushels of
oysters which your uncle sent I think we can
get up a fine supper. Don't you, my marvel
of a housekeeper? I hope you can, and hope,
too, that the good cheer it will provide will
help us to new and encouraging suggestions,
for, as hopeful as I always am, even *my* heart
is in my boots.

On every side gloom, dissatisfaction and
disappointment seem to have settled over all,
men and officers alike, because of the unsuc-
cessful termination of the Peace Conference
on board the *River Queen* on the fatal third.

THE HEART OF A SOLDIER

The anxious, despairing faces I see everywhere bespeak heavy hearts. Our commissioners knew that we were gasping our last gasp and that the Peace Conference was a forlorn hope. Because of the informality of the conference and my knowledge of Mr. Lincoln, his humanity, his broad nature, his warm heart, I did believe he would take advantage of this very informality and spring some wise, superhuman surprise which would, somehow, restore peace and in time insure unity. Now, heaven help us, it will be war to the knife, with a knife no longer keen, the thrust of an arm no longer strong, the certainty that when peace comes it will follow the tread of the conqueror.

I fear that you may need more help; so am sending over Bob. The mess-cook will come later.

Meantime, a Dios, and love,

YOUR SOLDIER.

Headquarters, January 28, 1865.

XXXVII

Written in Defeat, After the Battle of Five Forks

IT is long past the midnight hour and, like a boy, I have been reading over your dear, cheery letter, caressing the written page because it has been touched by your hand.

All is quiet now, but soon all will be bustle, for we march at daylight. Oh, my darling, were there ever such men as those of my division? This morning after the review I thanked them for their valiant services yesterday on the first of April, never to be forgotten by any of us, when, to my mind, they fought one of the most desperate battles of the whole war. Their answer to me was cheer after cheer, one after another calling out, "That's all right, Marse George, we only followed you." Then in the midst of these calls and silencing them, rose loud and clear dear old Gentry's voice, singing the old hymn which they all knew I loved:

THE HEART OF A SOLDIER

"Guide me, oh, thou great Jehovah,
Pilgrim through this barren land."

Voice after voice joined in till from all along the line the plea rang forth:

"Be my sword and shield and banner,
Be the Lord my righteousness."

I don't think, my Sally, the tears sounded in my voice as it mingled with theirs; but they were in my eyes and there was something new in my heart.

When the last line had been sung, I gave the order to march, proceeding to this point where I had expected to cross the Appomattox and rejoin the main army. While we were at a halt here orders came from General R. H. Anderson to report to him at Sutherland's Tavern.

Just after mailing my letter to you at Five Forks, telling you of our long, continuous march of eighteen hours and of the strenuous hours following those, where I had, because of exigent circumstances, been induced to fall back at daylight, I received a dispatch from the great Tyee telling me to "hold Five Forks at all hazards to prevent the enemy

You must have been up all night, my Prettice, to have made up and sent out such a basket of goodies and baked and buttered such a lot of biscuit and made so many jugs of coffee. My, I tell you, it all tasted good!—Page 123

from striking the south side railroad." This dispatch was in reply to one I had sent to him reporting the state of affairs and that the enemy were trying to get in between the army and my command, and asking that diversion be made at once or I should be isolated.

I had had all trains parked in the rear of Hatcher's Run and much preferred that position, but, from the General's dispatch, supposed that he intended sending reënforcements. I immediately formed line of battle upon the White Oak Road and set my men to throwing up temporary breastworks. Pine trees were felled, a ditch dug and the earth thrown up behind the logs. The men, God bless them, though weary and hungry, sang as they felled and dug. Three times in the three hours their labors were suspended because of attack from the front; but they as cheerily returned to their digging and to their "Annie Laurie" and "Dixie" as if they were banking roses for a festival.

Five Forks is situated in a flat, thickly wooded country and is simply a crossing at right angles of two country roads and a deflection of a third bisecting one of these an-

171

gles. Our line of battle, short as four small brigades front must be, could readily be turned on either flank by a larger attacking force. Do you understand, my dear? If not, you will some day, and you can keep this letter and show it to someone who will understand.

Well, I made the best arrangements of which the nature of the ground admitted, placing W. H. F. Lee's Cavalry on the right, Ransom's and Wallace's Brigades, acting as one and numbering about nine hundred, on the left; then Corse, Terry and Stuart, numbering about three thousand. Six rifled pieces of artillery were placed at wide intervals. Fitz Lee's Cavalry was ordered to take position on the left flank. About two o'clock in the afternoon Sheridan made a heavy demonstration with his cavalry, threatening also the right flank. Meantime Warren's Corps swept around the left flank and rear of the infantry line, attacking Ransom and Stuart behind their breastworks. Ransom sent word that the cavalry was not in position, and Fitz Lee was again ordered to cover the ground at once. I supposed it had been done, when suddenly the enemy in heavy infantry column appeared on our left and the attack became general. Ransom's horse was killed, falling with his rider under him. His Assistant Adjutant, General Gee, was killed. My dear, brave old friend, Willie Pegram was mortally wounded, falling within a few yards of me just after we had exchanged "Kla-how-ya, Tik-egh" (how are you, love to you) "and good luck." The captain of his—Pegram's —battery was killed.

I succeeded in getting a sergeant and enough men to man one piece; but after firing eight rounds the axle broke. Floweree's regiment fought hand to hand after all their cartridges had been used. The small cavalry force which had gotten into place gave way, and the enemy poured in on Wallace's left. Charge after charge was made and repulsed, and division after division of the enemy advanced upon us. Our left was turned; we were completely entrapped. Their cavalry, charging at a signal of musketry from the infantry, enveloped us front and right and, sweeping down upon our rear, held us as in a vise.

"Take this, Marse George," said one of my

boys earlier in the action, hastily thrusting a battle-flag into my hand. I took the flag, stained with his blood, sacred to the cause for which he fell, and, cheering as I waved it, called on my men to get into line to meet the next charge. Seeing this, a part of the famous old Glee Club, our dear old Gentry leading, began singing, "Rally round the flag, boys; rally once again." I rode straight up to where they were and joined in singing, "Rally Once Again," as I waved the blood-stained flag. And, my darling, overpowered, defeated, cut to pieces, starving, captured, as we were, those that were left of us formed front and north and south and met with sullen desperation their double onset. With the members of my own staff and the general officers and their staff officers we compelled a rally and stand of Corse's Brigade and W. H. F. Lee's Cavalry, who made one of the most brilliant cavalry fights of the war, enabling many of us to escape capture. Our loss in killed and wounded was heavy, and yet, my darling, with all the odds against us we might possibly have held out till night, which was fast approaching, but that our ammunition was exhausted.

We yielded to an overwhelming force, Sheridan's Cavalry alone numbering more than double my whole command, with Warren's Infantry Corps to back them.

Ah, my Sally, the triumphs of might are transient; but the sufferings and crucifixions for the right can never be forgotten. The sorrow and song of my glory-crowned division nears its doxology. May God pity those who wait at home for the soldier who has reported to the Great Commander! God pity them as the days go by and the sad nights follow.

The birds were hushed in the woods when I started to write, and now one calls to its mate "Cheer up—cheer up." Let's listen and obey the birds, my darling. Let's try to cheer up—cheer up. I remember that Milton said: "Those who best bear His mild yoke, they serve Him best." Let's bear and serve Him best, my darling wife.

Faithfully your

SOLDIER.

Exeter Mills, April 2, 1865.

XXXVIII

Three Hours Before Lee's Surrender at Appomattox

TO-MORROW, my darling, may see our flag furled forever. Jackerie, our faithful old mail-carrier, sobs behind me as I write. He bears to-night this—his last—message from me as "Our Cupid." First he is commissioned with three orders, which I know you will obey as fearlessly as the bravest of your brother soldiers. Keep up a stout heart. Believe that I shall come back to you and know that God reigns. After to-night you will be my whole command—staff, field officers, men—all. The second commission is only given as a precaution—lest I should not return or lest for some time I should not be with you.

Lee's surrender is imminent. It is finished. Through the suggestion of their commanding officers as many of the men as desire are permitted to cut through and join Johnston's army. The cloud of despair settled over all on the third, when the tidings came to us of the evacuation of Richmond and its partial loss by fire. The homes and families of many of my men were there, and all knew too well that with the fall of our Capital the last hope of success was over. And yet, my beloved, these men as resolutely obeyed the orders of their commanding officers as if we had captured and burned the Federal Capital.

The horrors of the march from Five Forks to Amelia Court House and thence to Sailor's Creek beggars all description. For forty-eight hours the man or officer who had a handful of parched corn in his pocket was most fortunate. We reached Sailor's Creek on the morning of the sixth, weary, starving, despairing.

Sheridan was in our front, delaying us with his cavalry (as was his custom) until the infantry should come up. Mahone was on our right, Ewell on our left. Mahone was ordered to move on, and we were ordered to stand still. The movement of Mahone left a gap which increased as he went on. Huger's

battalion of artillery, in attempting to cross
the gap, was being swept away when I pushed
on with two of my brigades across Sailor's
Creek.

We formed line of battle across an open
field, holding it against repeated charges of
Sheridan's dismounted cavalry. At about
three o'clock the infantry which Sheridan had
been looking for came up, completely hem-
ming us in. Anderson ordered me to draw off
my brigades to the rear and to cut our way
out in any possible manner that we could.
Wise's Brigade was deployed in the rear to
assist us, but was charged upon on all sides
by the enemy and, though fighting manfully
to the last, was forced to yield. Two of my
brigadiers, Corse and Hunton, were taken
prisoners. The other two barely escaped, and
my life, by some miracle, was spared. And
by another miracle, greater still, I escaped
capture. A squadron of the enemy's cavalry
was riding down upon us, two of my staff and
myself, when a small squad of my men recognized me and, risking their own lives, rallied
to our assistance and suddenly delivered a last
volley into the faces of the pursuing horse-

men, checking them but for a moment. But in that one moment we, by the speed of our horses, made our escape. Ah, my darling, the sacrifice of this little band of men is like unto that which was made at Calvary.

It is finished! Ah, my beloved division! Thousands of them have gone to their eternal home, having given up their lives for the cause they knew to be just. The others, alas, heartbroken, crushed in spirit, are left to mourn its loss. Well, it is practically all over now. We have poured out our blood and suffered untold hardships and privations all in vain. And now, well, *I* must not forget, either, that God reigns. Life is given us for the performance of duty, and duty performed is happiness.

It is finished—the suffering, the horrors, the anguish of these last hours of struggle. The glorious gift of your love will help me to bear the memory of them. In this midnight hour I feel the caressing blessing of your pure spirit as it mingles with mine. Peace is born.

From now forever only

YOUR SOLDIER.

Appomattox, April, 1865.

179

PART FIVE

Peace

AFTER the war had passed, and with it the necessity for separation from his dear one, the General's letters grew less frequent. He was seldom far from her side. A year they spent together in Canada during the exile which was enforced upon many of the leaders of the Lost Cause. Then, when the ban was finally lifted, the General returned with his pretty wife to face the problem that pressed heavily upon all Southerners— the disheartening task of rearing a new home on the ruins of the old. Their attempt was not altogether successful, but amid the surroundings of peace they found time to work out in practical form the dream of happiness which had come to them in darker days.

The letters in this part are written on occasional absences. They cover a period of ten years or more, extending almost to the time of the General's death, and to the end they breathe in every line his loyalty and devotion to the noble woman whose love had crowned his life.

XXXIX

*In Which the General Tells of a Trip to
Washington and a Visit With His
Old Friend, Grant*

SUCKLEY [1] and I arrived safely after an
interesting but, to me, sad trip, because
of the many sorrowful memories that it
brought back. Ingalls,[2] bless his old loyal
heart, met us at the train and took us up in the
Quartermaster's carriage. It is the first time
that I have ridden in one of Uncle Sam's
vehicles since I changed colors and donned
the gray, and now I ride, not as an owner but
as a *guest!* Again, my darling, there came to
me memories of the "has been" and "might
have been."

"Well, George," said Rufus, "this looks
kind of natural, doesn't it, old man?" but before I could reply, intuitively sensing what I

---

[1] Grant's surgeon.
[2] Grant's quartermaster.

was feeling, he continued hurriedly "and this rig is at your service all the time you are here."

The three of us had dinner together. Pitcher,[3] whom you've heard me speak of as "Old Jug," came over from his table and joined us at dessert. After dinner all four of us went to the theater to hear Billy Florence. We sent a line in to him from our box and when he came out he strode across the stage and, looking directly at us, said in his most tragic tone and manner: "The Lamb and the Lion shall lie down together," and then went on with his part. He knew and we knew, but the audience didn't. He played to us, too, all evening and never played better. After the play we went behind the scenes and had a charming visit with Mrs. Florence, who graciously gave her consent to Billy's going out to supper with us.

"And, by the way, General Pickett," said Mrs. Florence, "how is that beautiful Mrs. Edwards [4] with whom I saw you in Montreal and with whom you were so much in love and

[3] General T. Pitcher, U. S. A.
[4] Edwards was the assumed name of General Pickett and his wife during their exile in Canada.

who, come to think of it, won all our hearts?
Poor Ellen Tree was talking about her the
last time I saw her,— And how is that laughing, bright-eyed baby who made a drum of
himself and a prancing steed of everybody
else's cane? I can see him now, with his mass
of ringlets and his sparkling, laughing eyes.
He had just learned to walk and yet was
charging the enemy on his fiery steed, beating
an imaginary drum and blowing an imaginary
fife. It was the funniest thing I ever saw."

I told Mrs. Florence that we had returned
to the States, that little George could ride a
real horse now and beat a real drum, and that
I was just as much as ever in love with Mrs.
Edwards, who had become so attached to her
assumed name that she hated to give it up and
insisted that we should now and then call each
other "Mr. and Mrs. Edwards," to keep in
memory the sweet, all-belonging life we spent
with each other in Canada.

We had a fine steamed-oyster supper at
Harvey's and told stories and talked of old
times till after two o'clock.

I got up this morning just in time to go to
twelve o'clock breakfast at the Club with

Rufus. After breakfast we went, as arranged, to see Grant. I just can't tell you, my darling, about that visit. You'll have to wait till I see you to tell you how the warm-hearted modest old warrior and loyal old friend met me —how he took in his the hand of your heart-sore soldier—poor, broken, defeated—profession gone—and looking at him for a moment without speaking, said slowly: "Pickett, if there is anything on the top of God's green earth that I can do for you, say so." Just then his orderly apologetically brought in a card to him. "Tell Sheridan to go to ——!" "Yis, surh, I'll till him, surh." "And go there yourself!" "Yis, surh, I'll go, surh." Rufus, who was whistling over at the window, reiterated Grant's order, receiving from the orderly the same assurance, "Yis, surh, I'll till him, surh." While Sheridan was obeying Grant's order and going to his new station we three sat down and had a heart-to-heart conference. One listening would never have known that we had been on opposite sides of any question.

When I started to go Grant pulled down a cheque-book and said, "Pickett, it seems funny, doesn't it, that I should have any money to offer, but how much do you need?" "Not any, old fellow, not a cent, thank you," I said. "I have plenty." "But Rufus tells me that you have begun to build a house to take the place of the one old Butler burned and how can you build it without money; you do need some." "I have sold some timber to pay for it," I told him, and to show my appreciation and gratitude unobserved I affectionately squeezed his leg, when he called out, "Rufus, it's the same old George Pickett; instead of pulling my leg he's squeezing it."

Grant is going to take Rufus, Suckley and myself to ride this afternoon to show me the changes since I was last here, years ago.

To-morrow, if all goes well, I'll start back to what is worth more to me than *all* I've lost —my precious wife, who was as queenly and gracious and glorious as Mrs. Edwards in one room in a boarding house in exile as she was in Petersburg in a palatial home when her husband was the Department Commander and she had not only "vassals and slaves at her side," but the General Commanding and all his soldiers and our world at her feet.

YOUR DEVOTED SOLDIER.

XL

From New York After Refusing the Command of the Egyptian Army

SO, you would "leave it all to my better judgment," most wise Little One, and would not advise me, but after I had decided fully I was to read the mysterious sealed note —"not to be opened till after you have decided."

At the banquet last night I opened and read the letter and then passed it over to General E. P. Alexander, General Ingalls and Doctor Suckley. They all shook their heads disapprovingly. I pointed to the instructions, "Not to be opened till after you have decided," and said that I had already decided and the note only showed that we are "two souls with but a single thought."

Now, don't you know, my darling, that I knew your opinion before just as well as after I had read your sealed letter? Of course I knew that you did not want me to go and that,

188

as you prettily put it, "We've had glory enough, and war enough, with its hardships and separations and dangers, and now we just want each other forever and forevermore." Yes, my darling, we want each other and a home, with a spiked fence around it and a key to the road gate, for us alone,—just us, forever and forevermore.

My friends all think that I am making a great mistake in refusing this magnanimous offer of the Khedive. They hold that I am sacrificing my future and signing the death-warrant to ambition and success. General Alexander has accepted and will take command of the Egyptian armies; Egypt could not have a finer officer. Last night at the farewell dinner the Khedive's last telegram was handed to the Commissioner—"Forward Pickett at any cost." It was a most flattering compliment and I have asked permission to keep it for our boy. "The boy might think you were a brand of powder or a keg of nails," said Ingalls, who, by the way, is disgusted at my refusal. But, my beautiful wife, he has not you; and love such as yours is worth all the gold and glory of the universe.

THE HEART OF A SOLDIER

To-morrow I shall take the steamer for home without one regret for having decided as I have,—just you and I—just ourselves "forever and forever"—

YOUR SOLDIER.

XLI

A Letter From Turkey Island,[1] During a Short Absence of His Wife

IT is Thursday and the cottage is so empty—so desolate without my darling. Even Rufus feels the absence of its beautiful mistress and a few minutes ago, to show his sympathy for his lonesome master, brought and laid on my knee a little slipper which, if I did not know it belonged to my own fairy princess, would make me think that another Cinderella with a tinier foot had also forgotten the midnight hour. I gave no evidence of my appreciation of his effort to comfort me and Rufus trotted off and brought me the other slipper. "Good dog," I said, "good dog," patting him on the head. Then fondling the little slippers and putting them be-

---

[1] The old ancestral home called by the Federal soldiers Turkey Bend, is in Henrico Co., which is one of the original shires into which Virginia was divided in 1634.

side me I took up my pencil and pad to tell you all about it.

Presently, looking around, I saw Rufus planning to bring me everything in the room belonging to you. He has a lot of dog sense and I tried to make him understand that the slippers had been sufficiently effective in consoling me, but he would not be convinced until I whistled our song, "Believe me, if all those endearing young charms." Then trying to howl an accompaniment and failing, he wagged his tail, lay down at my feet and went to sleep.

Every day when I come in to dinner he trots up in front of your picture and barks till I take it down, then looking down at it barks again, while I encourage him, saying, "Tell her all about it, old man; tell her all about it." When he has told you about it he lies down beside it, his paw on the frame, wagging his tail and looking up at me till he thinks I have shown sufficient appreciation of his admiration and devotion to you, and then he jumps up and points and barks at the place on the rack from which it was taken until it is duly kissed and replaced. Oh, he's a great dog, little one, and great company for me, but both he and I and everything else are lonesome for you and we have promised our souls that when you come back we will vie with each other in our efforts to make you happy.

Already the hens have commenced laying again, the butter is piling up to be made into cakes and good things. Your new little calf is a beauty, but I shall send him off and sell him before you get back, for you would never allow him to be separated from his mother and would let him go on extracting her milk till he was a man—you great tender-hearted darling! The corn and wheat are beautiful, the vegetables fine and the flowers we planted all breathe of your purity and sweetness. The cutting from the Poe rosebush which Mrs. Allen gave us is full of buds; so you see everything above the ground and in the ground at our Turkey Island home is waiting for your blessing.

This morning I took my gun and Rufus and killed five partridges and two rabbits. I gave one rabbit to Mr. Sims and one to Uncle Tom. The birds I sent to Lizzie. As I was coming on home I stopped and rested in the cool and calm of the forest beside the old gray broken monument where we have so often made love and told each other fairy tales and wandered about and made thought pictures of our William and Mary Randolph, who erected it away back in 1771. I wonder, little one, if from their celestial home they can see the picturesque beauty which I see and which I wish I could put into words. Do you remember the inscription on one of the sides of the monument?—"The foundation of this pillar was laid in 1771, when all the great rivers of this country were swept by inundations never before experienced, which changed the face of nature and left traces of their violence that will remain for ages!" As I read over this inscription I feel sorry that the thought to erect a monument to commemorate any kind of disaster should ever have been born. Time's soothing wings bless always, and not only have the ravages of the flood which this monument was erected to commemorate been long ago forgotten, but the memories of ravages and horrors of a yesterday far, far more terrible are, thank God, being effaced.

The birds are nesting and songs are being born just where Butler's vandals mutilated and broke off the top of this monument, hunting for hidden treasure. Some of the seeds which the mother birds carried to their young have fallen by the wayside and taken root and now out of the jagged, broken top grow a greenery of unknown vines and plants and flowers. The old colonial home of my forefathers, with its rare old mahoganies and paintings, which Butler sacked and desecrated and then burned, has been replaced by a sweet little cottage home built by ourselves, all our very own, and consecrated to love and contentment, with furnishings so simple and plain that we are not afraid of using them.

No, my sweetheart, we don't want any monuments to mark any of the woes and horrors of the past. We must build one of hope and faith and peace and mercy and joy, the foundation of which is already laid in our hearts.

Listen—I hear old Sims' step on the porch. I hear him knocking his pipe against the pillars—so, á Dios. He will tell me the same old stories over again and I shall listen and laugh as though I heard them for the first time—dear old Sims.

Good night—sweet dreams. Angels guard you while I hear of Lafayette and Nelson and Marshall, through the clouds of old Sims' tobacco smoke for the hundredth, yes, thousandth time.

Your lonesome
SOLDIER.

XLII

Concerning a Slight Illness and the Business Troubles of a Soldier

Y OU are always right, my darling Sally, and your husband is only right when he is guided by you. Pretty generally he listens to his oracle and when he doesn't he wishes to the Lord he had. The morning I left, when you urged that I wear the suit I had been wearing and I claimed that I hadn't time to change—"Then please take it with you and change on the boat," you plead. Well, dearest, I was mean. I wouldn't and I didn't and your obstinate soldier was not out of sight of the sweet lone figure standing on the wharf waving to him the love signals and the Godspeed of our code before he was abusing himself as an ingrate in refusing anything that the sweetest, most beautiful woman and the best wife in the world could ask of him— "Well, dem dat dances is 'bleeged ter pay de fiddler," and your husband is paying—he is being punished, for he caught cold on the boat, had a chill, followed by sore throat and pain in limbs and back.

I stopped only a day in Petersburg to see our agent there, then came over here, went to the Exchange and went directly to bed and sent for Dr. Beal. He has been very attentive, coming twice a day. Julia and Wash took me in charge at once and, as usual, are as good as gold, and so is everyone, as to that, but each and all in turn prescribe a *sure* remedy and *urge* my taking it. Wash insists upon rubbing me with "turkentime en den puttin' on a hot ingun poultice, en 'pon top er dat drinkin' a good hot scotch," declaring "dey'll sho' en mingulate up wid one-an-nudder en do de business en bre'k up dis 'fluenza dat's got 'session er you, Marse George. Don't you go projickin' wid doctor's medicines; pills is dang'us en dey ain't gwine ter oust no 'fluenzas, dey jes' gwine ter upset en sturbulate de balance er yo' body dat ain' got de 'fluenza in it en mek dat part sick, too. Ef Miss Sally wuz here she'd say, 'Wash, you suttinly is right—g'long fetch up a nice hot scotch en git one fer yo'se'f while youse down dar gittin' yo Marse George's. Lord, I knows Miss Sally."

That settled it and I compromised on the hot scotch—but I was firm and would not yield to Julia's entreaties to be permitted to bring me Mrs. Marshall's flannel petticoat to wrap around my throat. "What would the judge say?" I asked. "De Jedge, Marse George?—De Jedge ain' 'bleeged ter know nuttin' 't all bout it. Needer him ner needer Miss Sally, nuther. Dem whar's robbed, en don' know dey's robbed, ain' robbed, Marse George, en ain' no wusser off ef dey had dan ef dey hadn't," she argued—but I was adamant; her arguments were of no avail. She "curchied" her thanks for the silver piece I gave her and left me with the compliment that I "sho' was one bridegroom-husband—allus honeymoonin' wid my own queen bee, wedder wid her er widout her, en dat Miss Sally ought ter be one proud white lady"—Is she?—bless her!

Yesterday when I wrote I did not tell you how sick I had been or was, nor how lonesome, nor how I longed for your soothing, gentle touch, your ministering care. I should only have made you anxious. You could not have come to me. Oh, my sweetheart, I think of you all the time, and I swear every time I leave you, that I'll never leave you again, that if business calls I must take my darling with me. If I could only lay the treasures of the universe at your tiny little feet.

But this business, I'm afraid, will not earn my cough drops or your violets and, oh darling, it *is* such a crucifixion. You don't know how abhorrent it is to me. I spur myself on all the time with this thought, that it is for my darling. The day I came up on the boat, I took out two policies, one for $7,000 and one for $10,000. The men were both old soldiers belonging to my dear old division and one of them said they had to run me down and almost tie me to make me insure their lives. You know, dear, I can't do it. I'd sooner face a cannon than ask a man to take out a policy with me. Your soldier is *nothing but a soldier;* the war is over and he is no more account. The company tells me that my agents must do the soliciting, but I'll feel like a thief to take a commission on what they have worked for and earned.

Yesterday when I came through Petersburg I went, as I told you, to our office. J. B. B., our company's agent, was sitting with his chair tilted back—foot on the table, smoking a bad smelling pipe and reading "Macaria." "Hello, General, hello," he said, not rising. "Sent in six policies this week, old man." "On your familiarity or courtly manners—which?" "Neither, old man, on gall, gall, old man, gall and grub. Come, have a drink —ever read 'Macaria'?" With the most studied politeness and coldness I declined his offer and in my most dignified manner asked permission to look over the company's books. "Come, what's eating you, old man?" he asked, bringing his chair down with a bang and slapping me on the back. Then he profanely informed me that I'd have to unbuckle a few holes and thaw out if I wanted to paint the monkey's tail sky-blue.

Alas, little one, I am afraid your Soldier isn't much of an artist. He longs to give his precious wife all the luxuries and comforts and everything that is beautiful—but he can't thaw out, my darling, and he can't paint that monkey's tail sky-blue, and, sweetheart, it makes me crawl and creep to be associated with artists who can. I was wondering as I came over whether it would be better to send our boy to West Point or get him a paint-brush. We have time to decide that, how-ever, for he is just a little over eleven.

Here comes the Colonel and "old Mistiss," and by the way, everybody sends love and messages to you and our boy.

Now, my own beautiful wife, don't be anx-ious about me, and forgive this long, rambling letter.

It's snowing hard—I mean, easy. The snow is "beautiful" but I'm so homesick for you.

Your loving, good-for-nothing
SOLDIER.

XLIII

*On the Occasion of the Memorial Services in
Honor of Those who died at Gettysburg*

ALL the way to the station, my darling, I
was asking myself whether I was right
in yielding to your solicitations and leaving
our sick child, with all the resulting care
and responsibility resting on your ever-brave
shoulders. And once, sweetheart, after thinking very seriously over it I was almost tempted
to turn and go back, when the appealing words
of your voice echoed through my soul. "Even
if I knew our child would die while you were
gone, I would not have you neglect *this call*
to honor your boys whom you led to their
death." And, instead of turning back I said:
"Drive faster, please, John David; I wouldn't
miss my train for anything."—You blessed
little sermon!

I made the train in plenty of time and your
mother, to whom I had telegraphed at Ivor,

came to the station, bringing the good tidings that your brother was out of danger. I did not tell her that our little George was ill, lest it might make her anxious, and I knew that her duty was beside her sick boy, your brother.

I would have been so thankful if you, my sweet, beautiful bride, and our precious little "war-baby" *could* have come with me. Everybody asks about you and the boy and sends love and expresses sorrow that you could not come. A delegation of my old soldiers met me at the station and, though some of our relatives had prepared to have us with them, I agreed to the arrangement of the Committee and the demand of the Governor and was taken to the Executive Mansion as the guest of the State.

All the evening and the next morning until it was time to form, old comrades came in, in groups and single file. They told of their experiences, officers and privates alike, discussed the Pennsylvania campaign and the three days' fight, their voices falling to a whisper as they spoke of those whose memory we had come to honor—our gallant dead at Gettysburg—our

THE HEART OF A SOLDIER

brave boys who gave "their last full measure of devotion" to duty.

I had been made Chief Marshal—a sad, solemn, sacred office for me—of all the Army. Such love, such reverence was Christ-born. You cannot conceive of it. From the old Market to the Cemetery of Hollywood the streets, sidewalks, windows and housetops were crowded. There must have been twelve thousand people at Hollywood. Such a demonstration of devotion and sympathy was, I think, never before witnessed on earth. Think of it, my darling, so penetrating, so universal a oneness of love and respect and reverence existed that there was a stillness, an awesomeness, save for those necessary sounds—the clanking of swords, the tramp of horses and the martial tread of men keeping time with funeral marches—the solemn requiem. No cheers, no applause, only loving greetings from tear-stained faces, heads bent in reverence, clasped hands held out to us as we passed along. As I saw once more the courage-lit faces of my brave Virginians, again I heard their cry—"We'll follow you, Marse George!" From their eternal silence those who marched heroically to death looked down upon us yesterday and were sad. My darling, you cannot know—no, you cannot know!

As I clasped the hand of one after another of those who crowded around me I was greeted with the words—"My husband was killed at Gettysburg." "My son is lying there among the dead"—"My brother was with you there and he has just come back to me"—so many crushed hearts filling my heart with grief. Oh, my Sally, if the cry of my soul had been voiced it would have been the echo of that at Gethsemane.

After the services General Joseph R. Anderson had a number of us old fellows come to his house and as we stood around his sumptuous board the solemnity of the scene was almost like that of the Lord's Supper. Though we were old soldiers, neither the march nor the battle was mentioned. The only war-time reference was that some of my men called me by the old war-time title, "Marse George." Among the guests were some of our West Point comrades whose only vocation, like mine, was war. Our tents are folded now and we parted, going off, each to

THE HEART OF A SOLDIER

his work; one to the farm, another to the trade;
one to seek some position; one to one place,
one to another; and I to return to my beautiful
wife and my sick baby, my only joy and my
life, knowing that what is best will come.

YOUR LOVING SOLDIER.

XLIV

*Written while Away from Home after the
Death of his Youngest Boy*

POOR broken lily, I hated so to leave you.
The haunted look on your sweet, tired
face haunts my heart and I was almost tempted
to disobey the company's orders and not go.
The doctor said you were not strong enough
to come with your Soldier, that you were all
run down by your long watch, sleepless nights
and nursing, and then the transplanting of the
precious flower into the Father's garden at last
—having to give the boy back—was more
than you could bear. Ah, sweetheart, try to
be generous, too, and give him to the Heavenly
Father, being thankful for His having lent
him to you for so long. Dear, beautiful
mother of an angel, come, say "Thy will be
done" and try to recognize the wisdom of our
Lord. See, my lily, how well your Soldier
has learned his lesson. It was you who taught

him to believe—to look up and trust. Come, now—take your spelling book and let *him* teach *you* the Word.

How tenderly, loyally, reverently I do love you, my wife, and how I want to spare you every hurt. I'll be starting back when you get this. Love to our boy and tell him to look after his "dear mother" for his "dear father," that he is our little man and has got double duty to do from now on. Ask him to think about what he wants for his birthday. Anything *but a gun* he can have.

Think, my darling, nearly eleven years of perfect bliss—such happiness as man never had. God show me how to be worthy of such a wife.

The horses are at the door, my little one— I must say á Dios.

Lovingly and forever and ever,

YOUR SOLDIER.

THE END

PICKETT'S CHARGE AT GETTYSBURG

[Editorial Note]

PICKETT'S charge was the culminating point in the three days' struggle at Gettysburg. Directed against a force strongly entrenched and superior in numbers it failed; but in failing it made immortal the fame of all those who took part in it.

For two days and a half the battle had raged between the armies of Lee and Meade, the advantage being with neither side, when at one o'clock in the afternoon of the third day Lee massed his forces on Seminary Ridge and prepared for a final assault upon the Union position. The attack was begun with a tremendous artillery duel which shook the surrounding hills. It lasted two hours. The Federal guns then ceased their fire, and Lee ordered the advance of the attacking columns.

This force consisted of Pickett's and Pettigrew's divisions, the brunt of the assault falling upon Pickett. At the order, the columns moved forward as on dress parade, their ranks unbroken, their arms glistening in the July sun. As they advanced, however, the Union artillery which had appeared to be silenced opened upon them with shot and shell, tearing great holes in the lines, and as they came nearer the men were met with a rain of canister and shrapnel. In the face of this terrific fire they did not falter. It was not until they came within striking distance of the Union line, when a flame of musketry burst forth before which nothing could live, that their ranks broke and, although a handful of men led by Armistead crossed the Union works, the remainder of the glory-crowned division were forced to retire.

Some idea of the decimating character of this assault may be gained from the fact that out of more than 5000 men in Pickett's division who started on the mile long march across the field of death but 1500 returned. In the two divisions that made up the attacking column over 5000 men were lost. Two of Pickett's brigadiers were killed, the other wounded; and but one field officer in his command came out of the battle unhurt. In one of his letters in this volume the general gives a more detailed account of the losses among his officers.

The charge of Pickett and his men has been made the basis of much unfavorable criticism, directed chiefly against the commanding general of the Southern forces and his chief lieutenants at Gettysburg. In this criticism Pickett has taken no part, although he states repeatedly in the letters to his wife that if promised supports had materialized the attack would have been successful. It is generally admitted that the brigades of Wilcox and Perry which should have supported Pickett were slow in starting and became separated from the main attacking body, rendering it no assistance.

In his first official report to General Lee after the battle, Pickett pointed out without reserve the circumstances that were responsible for the disastrous result.

THE HEART OF A SOLDIER

Lee, however, requested him to withdraw this report. His letter so doing is to be found in War Records (Volume 27, Part 3, Page 1075). It reads as follows:

General George E. Pickett, Commanding, &c. You and your men have crowned themselves with glory; but we have the enemy to fight, and must carefully, at this critical moment, guard against dissensions which the reflections in your report would create. I will, therefore, suggest that you destroy both copy and original, substituting one confined to casualties merely. I hope all will yet be well.

I am, with respect, your obedient servant,

R. E. Lee, General.

In accordance with Lee's wish, General Pickett withdrew and destroyed his report of the engagement. Furthermore, he looked upon Lee's suggestion as a command that was binding upon him for all time and he has never divulged the contents of this report, except in the letter to his wife (written before Lee's request was made) which appears in this volume on page 97. In view, however, of the General's sense of obligation in this matter, Mrs. Pickett feels that the details of the battle as reported therein should be withheld from publication and accordingly this section of the letter is omitted, as stated in footnote on page 100.

General Lee has been criticized for ordering the attack on Cemetery Ridge with an inadequate force and under conditions that made its failure probable. In explanation of his action, Lee said in his report (War Records,

Volume 27, Part 2, page 321) that his batteries "having nearly exhausted their ammunition in the protracted cannonade that preceded the advance of the infantry, were unable to reply, or render the necessary support to the attacking party. Owing to this fact, which was unknown to me when the assault took place, the enemy were enabled to throw a strong force of infantry against our left, already wavering under a concentrated fire of artillery from the ridge in front, and from Cemetery Hill on the left."

Elsewhere he describes the formation which took place in Pickett's charge, as follows:

"General Longstreet ordered forward the column of attack, consisting of Pickett's and Heth's divisions, in two lines, Pickett on the right. Wilcox's brigade marched in rear of Pickett's right, to guard that flank, and Heth's was supported by Lane's and Scales' brigades, under General Trimble."

General Longstreet has described the charge as seen under his own eyes in these words:

"I dismounted to relieve my horse and was sitting on a rail fence watching very closely the movements of the troops. . . . Pickett had reached a point near the Federal lines. A pause was made to close ranks and mass for the final plunge. The troops on Pickett's left, although advancing, were evidently a little shaky. I was watching the troops supporting Pickett and saw plainly they could not hold together ten minutes longer. I called his (Colonel Freemantle's) attention to the wavering condition of the two divisions of the Third Corps and said they would not hold, that Pickett would strike and be crushed, and the attack would be a failure. As the division threw itself against the Federal line Garnett fell and expired. The Confederate flag was planted in the Federal line, and immediately Armistead fell mortally wounded at the feet of the Federal soldiers. The wavering division then seemed appalled, broke their ranks and retired.

"The only thing Pickett said of his charge was that he was distressed at the loss of his command. He thought he should have had two of his brigades that had been left in Virginia; with them he felt that he would have broken the lines."

Suggested reading list:

Army Life: A Private's Reminiscences of the Civil War (20th Maine Volunteer Infantry) by Reverend Theodore Gerrish

Through Blood and Fire at Gettysburg: My Experiences with the 20th Maine Regiment on Little Round Top by General Joshua Lawrence Chamberlain

"Bayonet! Forward": My Civil War Reminiscences by General Joshua Lawrence Chamberlain

Soul of the Lion: A Biography of General Joshua Lawrence Chamberlain by Willard Wallace

The Passing of the Armies: The Last Campaign of the Armies by General Joshua Lawrence Chamberlain

The Attack and Defense of Little Round Top, Gettysburg, July 2, 1863 by Oliver W. Norton

Sickles the Incredible: A Biography of General Daniel Edgar Sickles by W. A. Swanberg

The Life and Letters of General George Gordon Meade by George Meade

A Diary of Battle: The Personal Journals of Colonel Charles S. Wainwright 1861-1865 edited by Allan Nevins

"Over a Wide, Hot ... Crimson Plain", The Struggle For The Bliss Farm by Elwood Christ

High Tide at Gettysburg: The Campaign in Pennsylvania by Glenn Tucker

Crisis at the Crossroads: The First Day at Gettysburg by Warren Hassler

The Killer Angels: A Novel About the Four Days of Gettysburg by Michael Shaara

The Great Invasion of 1863 or General Lee in Pennsylvania by Jacob Hoke

At Gettysburg or What a Girl Saw and Heard of the Battle: A True Narrative by Tillie (Pierce) Alleman

Gettysburg Sources: 3 Volumes, compiled by James L. McLean, Jr. and Judy W. McLean

The History of the Fighting Fourteenth: 14th Brooklyn State Militia compiled by C. Tevis and D. R. Marquis

Major-General John Frederick Hartranft: Citizen, Soldier and Pennsylvania Statesman by A. M. Gambone

The Civil War Letters of Dr. Harvey Black: A Surgeon with Stonewall Jackson edited by Glenn L. McMullen

Historical Record of the First Maryland Infantry by Charles Camper and J. W. Kirkley

The Baltimore and Ohio (Railroad) in the Civil War by Festus Summers

The History of the Tenth Massachusetts Battery of Light Artillery in the War of the Rebellion by John Billings

Whatever You Resolve To Be: Essays on Stonewall Jackson by A. Wilson Greene

Lee: A Biography by Clifford Dowdey

Pickett and His Men by LaSalle Corbell Pickett

A Texan in Search of a Fight: Being the Diary and Letters of a Private Soldier in Hood's Texas Brigade by John C. West

A Lieutenant of Cavalry in Lee's Army by George Beale

Letters of a Confederate Officer to His Family During the Last Year of the War of Secession by Richard Corbin

Death of a Nation: The Story of Lee and His Men at Gettysburg by Clifford Dowdey

Four Years in the Saddle by Colonel Harry Gilmor

Return to Bull Run: The Campaign and Battle of Second Manassas by John Hennessy

Confederate Monuments at Gettysburg: The Gettysburg Battle Monuments by David Martin

To the Gates of Richmond: The Peninsula Campaign by Stephen Sears

Mine Eyes Have Seen The Glory: The Civil War in Art by Harold Holzer and Mark E. Neely Jr.

All of the above titles are available from the Publisher:
Stan Clark Military Books
915 Fairview Avenue
Gettysburg, Pennsylvania 17325
(717) 337-1728